LEISURE
ARTS
the art of everyday living
www.leisurearts.com

Best of Fons & Porter

ScraP Quilts

FONS & PORTER STAFF
Editors-in-Chief Marianne Fons and Liz Porter

Editor Jean Nolte
Assistant Editor Diane Tomlinson
Managing Editor Debra Finan
Technical Writer Kristine Peterson

Art Director Tony Jacobson

Editorial Assistant Cinde Alexander
Sewing Specialist Cindy Hathaway

Contributing Photographers Craig Anderson, Dean Tanner, Katie Downey
Contributing Photo Assistant DeElda Wittmack

Publisher Kristi Loeffelholz
Advertising Manager Cristy Adamski
Retail Manager Sharon Hart
Web Site Manager Phillip Zacharias
Customer Service Manager Tiffiny Bond
Fons & Porter Staff Peggy Garner, Shelle Goodwin, Kimberly Romero, Laura Saner, Karol Skeffington, Yvonne Smith, Natalie Wakeman, Anne Welker, Karla Wesselmann

New Track Media LLC
President and CEO Stephen J. Kent
Chief Financial Officer Mark F. Arnett
President, Book Publishing W. Budge Wallis
Vice President/Publishing Director Joel P. Toner
Vice President Consumer Marketing Dennis O'Brien
Vice President, Production & Technology Derek W. Corson
Circulation Susan Sidler
IT Manager Denise Donnarumma
Group Marketing Manager Nicole McGuire
New Business Manager Lance Covert

Our Mission Statement
Our goal is for you to enjoy making quilts as much as we do.

LEISURE ARTS STAFF
Editor-in-Chief Susan White Sullivan
Quilt and Craft Publications Director Cheryl Johnson
Special Projects Director Susan Frantz Wiles
Senior Prepress Director Mark Hawkins
Imaging Technician Stephanie Johnson
Publishing Systems Administrator Becky Riddle
Mac Information Technology Specialist Robert Young

President and Chief Executive Officer Rick Barton
Vice President and Chief Operations Officer Tom Siebenmorgen
Vice President of Sales Mike Behar
Director of Finance and Administration Laticia Mull Dittrich
National Sales Director Martha Adams
Creative Services Chaska Lucas
Information Technology Director Hermine Linz
Controller Francis Caple
Vice President, Operations Jim Dittrich
Retail Customer Service Manager Stan Raynor
Print Production Manager Fred F. Pruss

Library of Congress Control Number: 2010941390
ISBN-13/EAN: 978-1-60900-110-0

10 9 8 7 6 5 4 3 2 1

We're thrilled to bring you this collection of some of our very favorite scrap quilts! The projects we've included are among our most popular of all time. You'll find challenging as well as easy patchwork, plus dashes of lovely appliqué. Enjoy the beautiful photography as you browse through the pages to find the quilt that's just right for you. Whether you are a batik-lover, a traditionalist, or a fan of contemporary fabric choices, you'll find plenty to love. You'll also appreciate our trademarked Sew Easy lessons that will guide you via step-by-step photography through any project-specific special techniques. We predict you'll have a hard time choosing only one project to add to your to-do list!

Happy quilting,

Marianne & Liz

Techniques

General Instructions **166**

118

138

152

Granny's Stars

Designer Nancy Mahoney used her collection of delightful 1930s reproduction prints to make this quilt. The colors are pretty and fresh, yet authentic to the period.

PROJECT RATING: INTERMEDIATE
Size: 76" × 94"
Blocks: 12 (16") blocks

MATERIALS

NOTE: Fabrics in the quilt shown are from the Granny's Treasures fabric collection by Nancy Mahoney for P&B Textiles.

5¾ yards cream solid for background

21 fat quarters★ assorted light, medium, and dark prints in green, lavender, blue, pink, orange, and yellow for blocks and yo-yos

¼ yard light green print for blocks and border corners

1 yard dark green print for blocks and appliqué

1¼ yards brown print for border corners, sashing squares, and binding

¼ yard medium pink print for appliqué

½ yard red print for blocks and appliqué

Paper-backed fusible web

5¾ yards backing fabric

Full-size quilt batting

★fat quarter = 18" × 20"

Cutting

Measurements include ¼" seam allowances. Border strips are exact length needed. You may want to make them longer to allow for piecing variations. Patterns for Petals, Leaves, and Yo-Yo Circle are on page 11. Follow manufacturer's instructions for using fusible web.

From cream solid, cut:

- 7 (10½"-wide) strips. Piece strips to make 2 (10½" × 74½") side borders and 2 (10½" × 56½") top and bottom borders.
- 2 (5¼"-wide) strips. From strips, cut 12 (5¼") squares. Cut squares in half diagonally in both directions to make 48 quarter-square D triangles.
- 7 (4½"-wide) strips. Cut strips in half to make 14 (4½" × 20") strips for strip sets.
- 28 (2½"-wide) strips for strip sets. From 18 strips, cut 31 (2½" × 16½") I rectangles and 16 (2½" × 4½") H rectangles. Cut remaining strips in half to make 20 (2½" × 20") strips for strip sets.
- 9 (1¼"-wide) strips. From strips, cut 48 (1¼" × 3⅜") C rectangles and 48 (1¼" × 2⅝") B rectangles.

From each of 3 dark print fat quarters, cut:

- 3 (5¼"-wide) strips. From strips, cut 8 (5¼") squares. Cut squares in half diagonally in both directions to make 32 quarter-square D triangles.

From 1 dark print fat quarter, cut:

- 3 (2⅞"-wide) strips. From strips, cut 16 (2⅞") squares. Cut squares in half diagonally to make 32 half-square E triangles.

From each of 3 medium print fat quarters, cut:

- 2 (4½"-wide) strips. From strips, cut 4 (4½") F squares.

From each of 3 light print fat quarters, cut:

- 3 (2⅝"-wide) strips. From strips, cut 16 (2⅝") A squares.

From remainder of fat quarters, cut a total of:

- 21 (2½"-wide) strips for strip sets.
- 36 Yo-Yo Circles.

  NOTE: Cut 4 yellow yo-yos to make flower centers.

From light green print, cut:

- 2 (2½"-wide) strips. Cut strips in half to make 4 (2½" × 20") strips. From 1 strip, cut 4 (2½") G squares. Remaining strips are for strip sets for border corners.

From dark green print, cut:

- 2 (2⅞"-wide) strips. From strips, cut 16 (2⅞") squares. Cut squares in half diagonally to make 32 half-square E triangles.
- 4 (1½"-wide) strips. From strips, cut 8 (1½" × 19½") strips for vines.
- 72 Leaves.

From brown print, cut:

- 4 (2½"-wide) strips. From 2 strips, cut 20 (2½") G squares. Cut remaining strips in half to make 4 (2½" × 20") strips for strip sets for border corners (1 is extra).
- 10 (2¼"-wide) strips for binding.

From medium pink print, cut:

- 16 Large Petals.

From red print, cut:

- 2 (2⅞"-wide) strips. From strips, cut 16 (2⅞") squares. Cut squares in half diagonally to make 32 half-square E triangles.
- 16 Small Petals.

Block Assembly

1. Join 1 (2½"-wide) print strip and 1 (4½"-wide) cream strip as shown in *Strip Set #1 Diagram*. Make 14 Strip Set #1. From strip sets, cut 96 (2½"-wide) #1 segments.

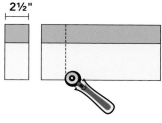

Strip Set #1 Diagram

2. Join 1 (2½"-wide) print strip and 2 (2½"-wide) cream strips as shown in *Strip Set #2 Diagram*. Make 7 Strip Set #2. From strip sets, cut 48 (2½"-wide) #2 segments.

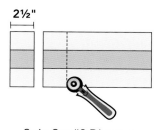

Strip Set #2 Diagram

3. Lay out 2 #1 segments and 1 #2 segment as shown in *Corner Unit Diagrams*. Join segments to complete 1 Corner Unit. Make 48 Corner Units.

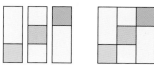

Corner Unit Diagrams

4. Choose 1 set of 4 matching print A squares, 8 matching print D triangles, 8 matching print E triangles, and 1 print F square.

5. Join 1 A square, 1 cream B rectangle, and 1 cream C rectangle as shown in *Square Unit Diagrams* to make 1 Square Unit.

Square Unit Diagrams

6. Lay out 1 Square Unit, 2 print D triangles, 1 cream D triangle, and 2 E triangles as shown in *Star Point Unit Diagrams*. Join to make 1 Star Point Unit. Make 1 set of 4 matching Star Point Units.

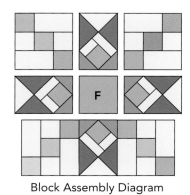

Star Point Unit Diagrams

7. Lay out 4 Corner Units, 1 set of 4 matching Star Point Units, and 1 F square as shown in *Block Assembly Diagram*. Join into rows; join rows to complete 1 block *(Block Diagram)*. Make 12 blocks.

Block Assembly Diagram

Block Diagram

Border Assembly

1. Fold dark green print strips in thirds; press and hand baste folds in place to prepare vines for appliqué.

2. Refer to *Sew Easy: Making Yo-Yos* on page 107 to make 36 yo-yos using assorted print circles.

3. Referring to quilt photo on page 7, arrange 4 Large and 4 Small Petals, 2 vines, and 18 Leaves on 1 side border strip. Appliqué using matching thread.

4. Appliqué 1 yellow yo-yo in center of flower and 8 assorted yo-yos along vine as shown. Repeat for remaining borders.

5. Join 1 (2½"-wide) light green print strip and 1 (2½"-wide) cream strip as shown in *Strip Set #3 Diagram*. Make 3 Strip Set #3. From strip sets, cut 16 (2½"-wide) #3 segments.

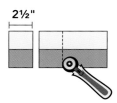

2½"

Strip Set #3 Diagram

6. Join 1 (2½"-wide) brown print strip and 1 (2½"-wide) cream strip as shown in *Strip Set #4 Diagram*. Make 3 Strip Set #4. From strip sets, cut 16 (2½"-wide) #4 segments.

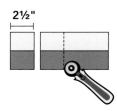

2½"

Strip Set #4 Diagram

7. Join 1 #3 segment and 1 #4 segment to complete 1 Four Patch Unit *(Four Patch Unit Diagrams)*. Make 16 Four Patch Units.

Four Patch Unit Diagrams

8. Lay out 4 Four Patch Units, 4 cream H rectangles, and 1 light green G square as shown in *Corner Unit Diagrams*. Join into rows; join rows to complete 1 Corner Unit. Make 4 Corner Units.

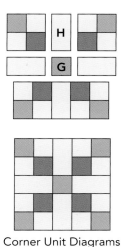

Corner Unit Diagrams

Quilt Assembly

1. Lay out blocks, cream I rectangles, and brown print G squares as shown in *Quilt Top Assembly Diagram* on page 10. Join into rows; join rows to complete quilt center.

2. Add appliquéd side borders to quilt center. Join 1 Corner Unit to each end of appliquéd top and bottom borders. Add borders to quilt.

Finishing

1. Divide backing into 2 (2⅞-yard) lengths. Cut 1 piece in half lengthwise to make 2 narrow panels. Join 1 narrow panel to each side of wider panel; press seam allowances toward narrow panels.

2. Layer backing, batting, and quilt top; baste. Quilt as desired. Quilt shown was quilted with flower designs in the blocks and border corners, and with meandering in the borders *(Quilting Diagram)*.

3. Join 2¼"-wide brown print strips into 1 continuous piece for straight-grain French-fold binding. Add binding to quilt.

TRIED & TRUE

Leaf prints from the Nature's Palette collection by Michele Scott for Lyndhurst Studio provide visual texture in our block.

Quilt Top Assembly Diagram

Quilting Diagram

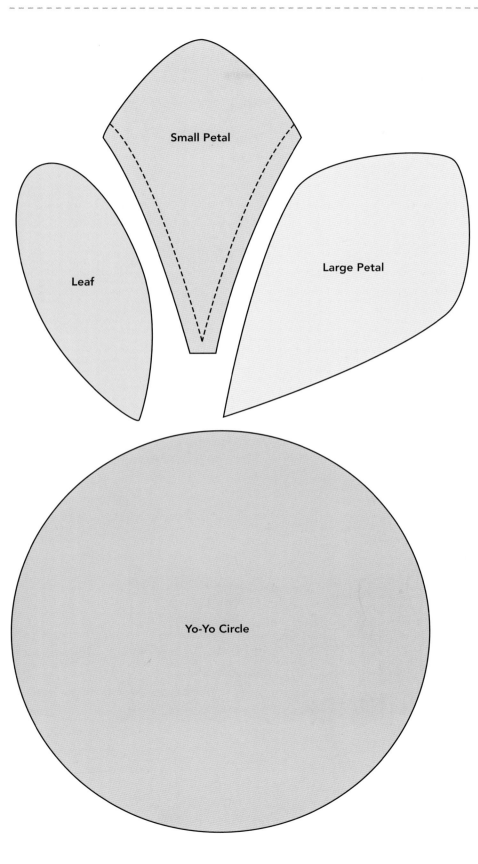

Small Petal

Leaf

Large Petal

Yo-Yo Circle

DESIGNER

A prolific quiltmaker and author of ten books, Nancy Mahoney is also a teacher and fabric designer. She enjoys making traditional quilts using new techniques that make quiltmaking easy and fun. Look for Nancy's latest book, *Treasures from the '30s*, in your local quilt shop. ✳

Artisan Star

Designer Patti Carey made this technicolor dream quilt using a variety of jewel tones combined with metallic golds. The center is constructed in rows rather than blocks and uses only Flying Geese units and squares, making this quilt quick and easy.

PROJECT RATING: EASY

Size: 94" × 112"

MATERIALS

NOTE: Fabrics in the quilt shown are from the Artisan's Palette and Heavy Metal collections by Ro Gregg for Northcott.

32 fat quarters★ assorted jewel-tone prints for quilt center and pieced border

3¼ yards black/gold marble for borders and binding

2½ yards cream/gold print for Flying Geese Units

2¾ yards black/gold print for Flying Geese Units

Quilt in a Day® Flying Geese Ruler (optional)

8⅝ yards backing fabric

King-size quilt batting

★fat quarter = 18" × 20"

Cutting

Measurements include ¼" seam allowances. Border strips are exact length needed. You may want to make them longer to allow for piecing variations.

From each fat quarter, cut:
- 1 (7½"-wide) strip. From strip, cut 6 (2½" × 7½") D rectangles.
- 1 (6½"-wide) strip. From strip, cut 2 (6½") C squares.
- 1 (3½"-wide) strip. From strip, cut 3 (3½") B squares.

From black/gold marble, cut:
- 11 (5½"-wide) strips. Piece strips to make 2 (5½" × 102½") side outer borders and 2 (5½" × 94½") top and bottom outer borders.
- 8 (2½"-wide) strips. Piece strips to make 2 (2½" × 84½") side inner borders and 2 (2½" × 70½") top and bottom inner borders.
- 11 (2¼"-wide) strips for binding.

From cream/gold print, cut:
- 24 (3½"-wide) strips. From strips, cut 142 (3½" × 6½") A rectangles. **Note:** If using Quilt in a Day® ruler for making Flying Geese, cut 8 (7½"-wide) strips. From strips, cut 36 (7½") squares. See *Sew Easy: Eleanor's Quick Flying Geese* on page 15 for assembly instructions.

From black/gold print, cut:
- 26 (3½"-wide) strips. From strips, cut 284 (3½") B squares. **Note:** If using Quilt in a Day® ruler for making Flying Geese, cut 9 (9"-wide) strips. From strips, cut 36 (9") squares. See *Sew Easy: Eleanor's Quick Flying Geese* on page 15 for assembly instructions.

Flying Geese Unit Assembly

(Follow these instructions if not using Eleanor's Quick Flying Geese method on page 15.)

1. Referring to *Diagonal Seams Diagrams*, place 1 black/gold print B square atop corner of 1 cream/gold print A rectangle. Stitch diagonally from corner to corner. Trim ¼" beyond stitching. Press open to reveal triangle.

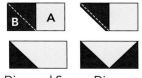

Diagonal Seams Diagrams

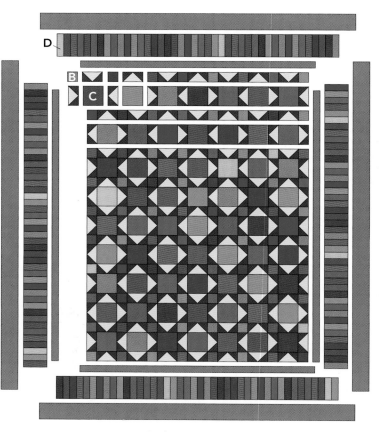

Quilt Top Assembly

2. Repeat on opposite end of rectangle to complete 1 Flying Geese Unit. Make 142 Flying Geese Units.

Quilt Assembly

1. Lay out B squares, C squares, and Flying Geese Units as shown in *Quilt Top Assembly Diagram.* Join into horizontal rows; join rows to complete quilt center.

2. Add side inner borders to quilt center. Add top and bottom inner borders to quilt.

3. Join 44 D rectangles to make 1 side border. Add border to quilt. Repeat for opposite side.

4. Join 42 D rectangles to make top border. Add border to quilt. Repeat for bottom border.

5. Add side outer borders to quilt center. Add top and bottom outer borders to quilt.

Finishing

1. Divide backing into 3 (2⅞-yard) pieces. Join panels lengthwise. Seams will run horizontally.

2. Layer backing, batting, and quilt top; baste. Quilt as desired. Quilt shown was outline quilted in the Flying Geese Units and has diamonds in the large squares.

3. Join 2¼"-wide black/gold marble strips into 1 continuous piece for straight-grain French-fold binding. Add binding to quilt.

DESIGNER

As Marketing Director for Northcott, Patti Carey enjoys playing with all the new fabrics her company produces. She loves to design quilts when new collections arrive, and hopes to inspire other quilters with her creations. ✳

Sew Easy™

Eleanor's Quick Flying Geese

Use the Quilt in a Day® Flying Geese Ruler to make dozens of Flying Geese units quickly and accurately for quilts such as *Artisan Star* on page 12.

1. To make 4 (3" × 6" **finished** size) Flying Geese units, cut 1 (7½") square of fabric for the larger "goose" triangles and 1 (9") square of fabric for the smaller "wing" triangles. Center the smaller square atop the larger square, right sides facing; press.

2. Draw a diagonal line across the squares; pin squares together. Stitch ¼" on each side of diagonal line; press to set seam. Cut on drawn line (*Photo A*). Press seam allowances toward larger triangles.

3. Place squares right sides together with opposite fabrics facing. Match up **outside** edges (*Photo B*). There will be a gap between the seams.

4. Draw a diagonal line across square, crossing the seams; pin. Stitch ¼" on each side of drawn line; press to set seam. Cut on drawn line (*Photo C*).

5. Clip vertical seam allowance midway between horizontal seams. Press seam allowances toward "wing" fabric, which was originally the larger square (*Photo D*).

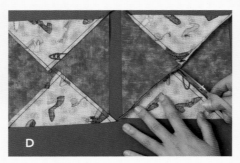

6. Line up the green dashed line on the Flying Geese ruler with the peak of the "goose" triangle; line up the green solid lines on the ruler with the angled stitching lines (*Photo E*). Cut along all sides of ruler to trim unit to correct size. Repeat for remaining Flying Geese unit.

Sew **Smart**™
Place the unit on a small cutting mat that you can rotate easily as you trim around the ruler. —Eleanor

AUTHOR

Well known as an author, teacher, and television host, Eleanor Burns has been creating Quilt in a Day® books, techniques, and tools since 1978. Eleanor's enthusiasm for quilting and her unique personality have gained her many thousands of fans worldwide. ✳

Turnstile

Kay Kingsley of Indiana designed her Turnstile block after seeing a small photo of a Pinwheel quilt in a catalog. She said, "I figured out how I wanted to stitch my block, and immediately went shopping to expand my 1930s fabric collection." Her quilt is made entirely from 2½"-wide strips, and would be a great Cutting Bee project (see page 162).

Size: 86" × 86"

Blocks: 36 (12") Turnstile blocks

MATERIALS

1½ yards white for block backgrounds

36 fat quarters★ assorted prints for blocks

2¼ yards green solid for sashing

⅜ yard pink print #1 for sashing squares

¾ yard pink print #2 for binding

7⅞ yards backing fabric

Queen-size quilt batting

★fat quarter = 18" × 20"

Cutting

Measurements include ¼" seam allowances.

From white fabric, cut:

- 18 (2½"-wide) strips. From strips, cut 288 (2½") A squares for block backgrounds.

From each fat quarter, cut:

- 5 (2½"-wide) strips. From strips, cut:
  4 (2½" × 6½") C rectangles,
  8 (2½" × 4½") B rectangles, and
  12 (2½") A squares.

From green solid, cut:

- 28 (2½"-wide) strips. From strips, cut 84 (2½" × 12½") sashing strips.

From pink print #1, cut:

- 4 (2½"-wide) strips. From strips, cut 49 (2½") sashing squares.

From pink print #2, cut:

- 9 (2¼"-wide) strips for binding.

Block Assembly

1. To make 1 block, choose 2 matching sets of 6 A squares and 2 B rectangles from print fabric for pinwheels. Choose 1 matching set of 4 B and 4 C rectangles from print fabric for block frame.

2. Referring to *Flying Geese Unit Diagrams* on page 18, place 1 white A square atop 1 B pinwheel fabric rectangle. Stitch diagonally from corner to corner as shown. Trim ¼" beyond

stitching. Press open to reveal triangle. Using the same method, stitch 1 A square to opposite end of rectangle to complete 1 Flying Geese Unit. Make 2 sets of 2 matching Flying Geese Units from pinwheel fabrics.

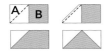

Flying Geese Unit Diagrams

3. Referring to *Block Frame Diagrams*, place 1 pinwheel fabric A square atop 1 block frame print B rectangle as shown. Stitch diagonally from corner to corner. Trim ¼" beyond stitching and press open to complete 1 Block Frame Unit. Make 2 sets of 2 matching Block Frame Units.

Block Frame Diagrams

4. Lay out pieces as shown in *Quadrant A Diagrams*. Join 2 contrasting A squares. Add Flying Geese unit to left side. Add Block Frame Unit to top. Add C rectangle to left side to complete 1 Quadrant A. Make 2 Quadrant A.

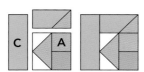

Quadrant A Diagrams

5. In the same manner, make 2 Quadrant B as shown in *Quadrant B Diagrams*.

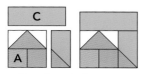

Quadrant B Diagrams

6. Lay out 2 Quadrant A and 2 Quadrant B as shown in *Block Assembly Diagram*. Join quadrants to complete 1 Turnstile block *(Block Diagram)*. Make 36 blocks.

Quadrant A Quadrant B

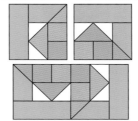

Quadrant B Quadrant A
Block Assembly Diagram

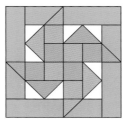

Block Diagram

Quilt Assembly

1. Referring to *Pre-Sashing Diagram*, add 1 green sashing strip to left side of 1 block. Join 1 pink sashing square to end of 1 green sashing strip. Join to top edge of block. Repeat for all blocks.

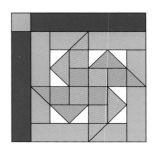

Pre-Sashing Diagram

2. Make bottom sashing row by joining 6 pink sashing squares and 6 green sashing strips. Make right side sashing row by joining 7 pink sashing squares and 6 green sashing strips.

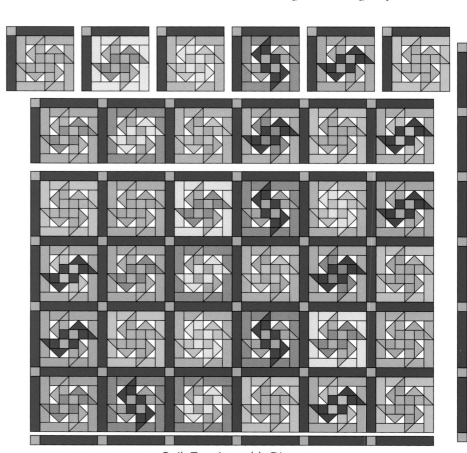

Quilt Top Assembly Diagram

3. Lay out blocks as shown in *Quilt Top Assembly Diagram*. Join blocks into rows; join rows.

4. Add bottom sashing row to quilt. Add right side sashing row.

Quilting and Finishing

1. Divide backing fabric into 3 (2⅝-yard) pieces. Divide 1 piece in half lengthwise. Join 1 wide panel to each side of 1 narrow panel to make quilt back. Remaining panel is extra and can be used to make a hanging sleeve.

2. Layer backing, batting, and quilt top; baste. Quilt as desired. Quilt shown was quilted with a diagonal grid in blocks and cables in sashing.

3. Join 2¼"-wide pink print #2 strips into 1 continuous piece for straight-grain French-fold binding. Add binding to quilt.

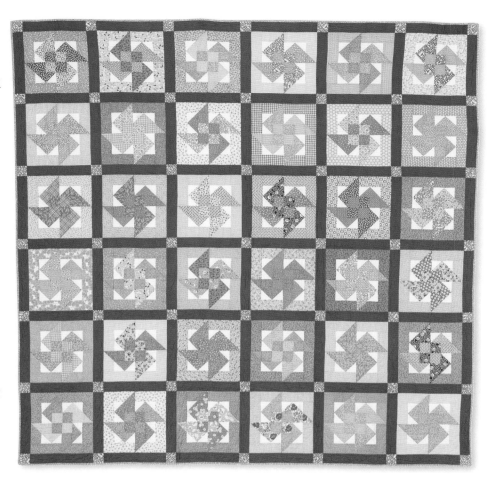

DESIGNER

Kay Kingsley loves teaching quilting and says, "My goal is to excite and motivate my students to step out of their box and see things in a new way." ✳

TRIED & TRUE

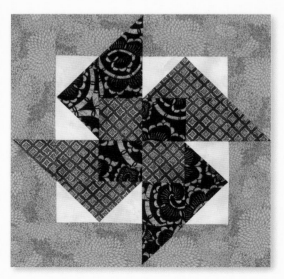

This dramatic version uses fabrics from the Indonesia collection by P&B Textiles.

Little Susan

Designer Loyce Saxton created this wallhanging featuring vintage dishtowel designs on quilt blocks. She used hand embroidery and color crayon techniques. Read *Coloring on Fabric* on page 23 to learn how.

PROJECT RATING: INTERMEDIATE
Size: 34" × 34"
Blocks: 4 (8") Little Susan blocks

MATERIALS

1¼ yards cream print for block backgrounds and inner border

½ yard blue print for corner triangles and binding

8 fat eighths★ assorted yellow, pink, green, and blue 1930s prints for sashing and outer border

1⅛ yards backing fabric

Freezer paper

Embroidery floss in flesh, light brown, blue, green, yellow, red, dark brown, pink, and black

Crayons in colors to match embroidery floss

Hand sewing needle for embroidery

Crib-size quilt batting

★fat eighth = 9" × 20"

Cutting

Embroidery patterns are on pages 23–25. Stitch diagrams are on page 23. Measurements include ¼" seam allowances. Border strips are exact length needed. You may want to make them longer to allow for piecing variations.

From cream print, cut:

• 2 (10½"-wide) strips. From strips, cut 4 (10½") squares for block backgrounds.

• 4 (4½"-wide) strips. From strips, cut 2 (4½" × 30½") top and bottom inner borders and 2 (4½" × 22½") side inner borders.

From blue print, cut:

• 2 (2½"-wide) strips. From strips, cut 20 (2½") A squares.

• 4 (2¼"-wide) strips for binding.

From each fat eighth, cut:

• 2 (2½"-wide) strips. From strips, cut 16 (2½") A squares for sashing and outer border. (You will have a few extra.)

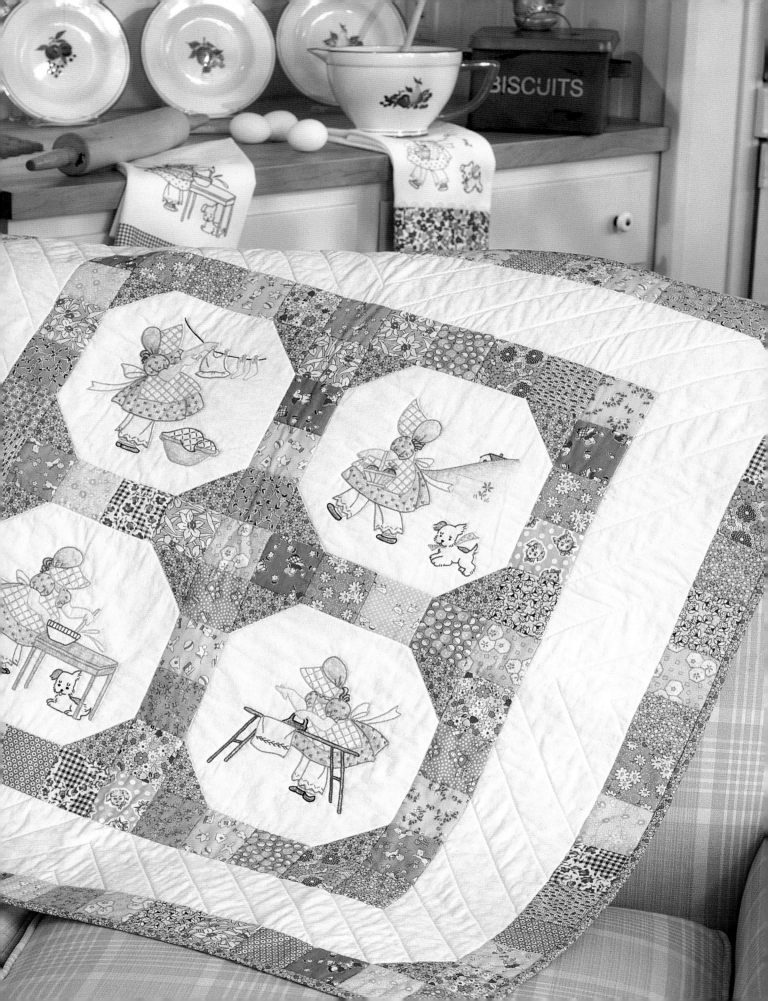

Block Assembly

1. Referring to *Coloring on Fabric* on page 23, transfer embroidery pattern to cream background square and color design.

2. Using two strands of embroidery floss and colors matching crayon work, outline stitch design. Use satin stitch for dog's eyes, lazy daisy stitch for leaves and flowers, French knots for dots, and featherstitch on towel.

3. Trim block to 8½".

4. Referring to *Diagonal Seams Diagrams*, place 1 blue print A square atop corner of embroidered block background, right sides facing. Stitch diagonally from corner to corner. Trim excess ¼" beyond stitching. Press open to reveal triangle. Repeat on remaining 3 corners to complete 1 block. Make 4 Little Susan blocks.

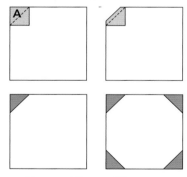

Diagonal Seams Diagrams

Quilt Assembly

1. Lay out blocks and assorted print A squares as shown in *Quilt Top Assembly Diagram*. Join into horizontal rows; join rows to complete quilt center.

2. Add cream side inner borders to quilt center. Add top and bottom inner borders to quilt.

3. Referring to *Quilt Top Assembly Diagram*, place 1 blue print A square atop corner of quilt center, right sides

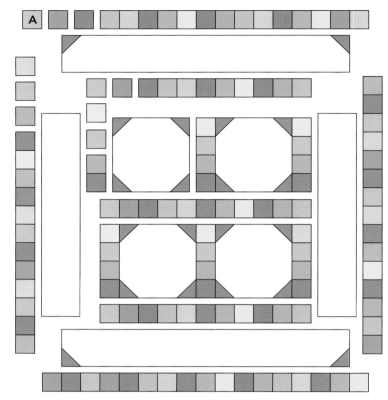

Quilt Top Assembly Diagram

facing. Stitch diagonally from corner to corner. Trim excess ¼" beyond stitching. Press open to reveal triangle. Repeat on remaining 3 corners.

Outer Border Assembly

1. Referring to *Quilt Top Assembly Diagram,* join 15 assorted print A squares to make side border. Make 2 side borders. Add borders to sides of quilt.

2. Join 17 assorted print A squares to make top border. Repeat for bottom border. Add borders to top and bottom of quilt.

Finishing

1. Layer backing, batting, and quilt top; baste. Quilt as desired. Quilt shown was quilted in the ditch in sashing and border squares, outline quilted around embroidered designs, and with diagonal lines in the inner border.

2. Join 2¼"-wide blue print strips into 1 continuous piece for straight-grain French-fold binding. Add binding to quilt.

DESIGNER

Loyce Saxton of La Grande, Oregon, carries on a family tradition of sewing by using her grandmother's treadle sewing machine and quilting hoop to make quilts for her children. Her pattern business, Yesterday's Charm, focuses on vintage designs. ✳

COLORING ON FABRIC

1. Pre-wash fabric to remove all chemicals.
2. Transfer design onto fabric.
3. Iron freezer paper to back of fabric to stabilize it for coloring.
4. Use regular crayons, and color directly onto the fabric. Color lightly and evenly until you achieve the desired shade.
5. Lay colored fabric face down on a paper towel. Iron back side of fabric with a hot, dry iron for 20–30 seconds. Keep iron moving in a circular motion.
6. If necessary, add more color and heat set again.
7. Remove freezer paper and stitch embroidery design.
8. Crayon work will fade a little when washed. If desired, add more color and heat set with a hot iron.

> ### Sew **Smart**™
> Coloring on fabric is a great way to give embroidery work a vintage hand-tinted look similar to the tinted embroidery kits that were sold in the 1920s through 1950s.
> —Marianne

Outline Stitch

French Knot

Featherstitch

Laisy Daisy

Satin Stitch

TRIED & TRUE

For the dish towel version of her
Little Susan designs, Loyce stitched one
with several colors of embroidery floss
and the other with red only for
a redwork look.

Lauren's Pinwheels

Alabama quilter Lauren Brooks loves bright, cheery fabrics, and pinwheels are her favorite quilt blocks. She combined these elements to stitch a charming quilt that any little girl would love. Simply alter your color scheme to make a quilt for a boy's room.

Size: 56" × 76"

Blocks: 35 (8") Pinwheel Blocks

MATERIALS

7 fat quarters★ assorted pink prints for blocks

9 fat quarters★ assorted yellow prints for blocks

1 yard pink print for sashing squares and binding

1 yard yellow floral print for blocks and border

1¾ yards white print for sashing

3½ yards backing fabric

Twin-size quilt batting

★Fat quarter = 18" × 20"

Cutting

Measurements include ¼" seam allowances. Border strips are exact length needed. You may want to cut them longer to allow for piecing variations.

From each pink fat quarter, cut:

• 2 (4⅞"-wide) strips. From strips, cut 6 (4⅞") squares. Cut squares in half diagonally to make 3 sets of 4 half-square triangles each for blocks.

From each yellow fat quarter, cut:

• 3 (4⅞"-wide) strips. From strips, cut 10 (4⅞") squares. Cut squares in half diagonally to make 5 sets of 4 half-square triangles each for blocks.

From pink print, cut:

• 3 (2½"-wide) strips. From strips, cut 48 (2½") squares for sashing squares.

• 7 (2¼"-wide) strips for binding.

From yellow floral print, cut:

• 1 (4⅞"-wide) strip. From strip, cut 8 (4⅞") squares. Cut squares in half diagonally to make 4 sets of 4 half-square triangles each for blocks.

• 7 (2½"-wide) strips. Piece strips to make 2 (2½" × 72½") side borders and 2 (2½" × 56½") top and bottom borders.

From white print, cut:

• 21 (2½"-wide) strips. From strips, cut 82 (2½" × 8½") sashing strips.

Block Assembly

1. Choose 2 sets of 4 matching triangles. Join 1 triangle from each set as shown in *Triangle-Square Diagrams*. Make 4 triangle-squares.

Triangle-Square Diagrams

2. Lay out triangle-squares as shown in *Block Assembly Diagram*. Join into rows; join rows to complete 1 Pinwheel block (*Block Diagram*). Make 35 Pinwheel blocks.

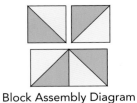

Block Assembly Diagram

Block Diagram

Quilt Assembly

1. Lay out blocks, sashing strips, and sashing squares as shown in *Quilt Top Assembly Diagram*. Join into rows; join rows to complete quilt center.
2. Add yellow print side borders to quilt center. Add yellow print top and bottom borders to quilt.

Quilting and Finishing

1. Divide backing fabric into 2 (1¾-yard) lengths. Cut 1 piece in half lengthwise. Join 1 narrow panel to each side of wider panel. Press seam allowances toward narrow panels. Seams will run horizontally.

2. Layer backing, batting, and quilt top; baste. Quilt as desired. Quilt shown was quilted with spirals in Pinwheel blocks and meandering in sashing and border.

3. Join 2¼"-wide pink print strips into 1 continuous piece for straight-grain French-fold binding. Add binding to quilt.

DESIGNER

Lauren Caswell Brooks suggests machine quilting all baby and children's quilts. She says, "Machine quilting will hold up better through multiple washings, and it is a speedy way to finish a quilt in time for a baby shower or a birthday party." ✳

Quilt Top Assembly Diagram

Sew *Easy*™

Pre-Sashing Blocks for Quicker Setting

When you make a quilt that has sashing strips and corner squares between the rows of blocks, the instructions usually tell you to construct two types of rows—block rows and sashing rows. Block rows consist of blocks alternating with sashing strips, and sashing rows consist of sashing strips alternating with sashing squares (sometimes called cornerstones). Once you get your rows assembled, you join them with long horizontal or vertical seams.

Our method of "pre-sashing" means you add sashing and sashing squares to the blocks ahead of time. This way, you avoid dealing with those long skinny rows of sashing and squares. Pre-sashing would work great for *Lauren's Pinwheels.*

1. Sew a sashing strip to the left side of a block as shown in *Diagram 1*. Press seam allowances toward the sashing strip. Repeat for all blocks.
2. Join 1 sashing square to 1 sashing strip as shown in *Diagram 2*. Press seam allowances toward the sashing strip. Repeat for all sashing squares and sashing strips.
3. Sew the sashing square/sashing strip unit to the top of the block as shown in *Diagram 3*. Repeat for all blocks.
4. Lay out pre-sashed blocks. To complete each row, sew a sashing square/sashing strip unit to the block at the right end of each row as shown in *Quilt Assembly Diagram*. Join rows.
5. Join sashing square/sashing strip units and single sashing square to make a sashing row for the bottom edge of the quilt. Join row to bottom of quilt.

Diagram 1

Diagram 2

Diagram 3

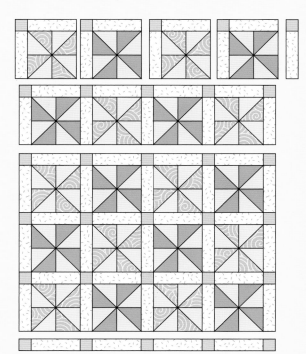

Quilt Assembly Diagram

Antique Fans

Make this quintessential 1940s quilt quickly using our easy Fan Blade technique.
Get out your fat quarter collection and start stitching!

PROJECT RATING: CHALLENGING
Size: 78" × 91"
Blocks: 20 (14") Fan blocks

MATERIALS

25 fat quarters★ assorted 1930s
reproduction prints in blue, red,
yellow, pink, green, and orange
5¼ yards blue solid for fan centers,
sashing, borders, and binding
4¾ yards cream solid for background
Template plastic
Tailor's chalk
7½ yards backing fabric
Queen-size quilt batting
★fat quarter = 18" × 20"

Cutting

Measurements include ¼" seam allowances.
Patterns for templates are on page 33.
From each fat quarter, cut:

- 2 (4¾"-wide) strips. From strips, cut
16 Fan Blades as shown in *Fan Blade
Cutting Diagram.*

From blue solid, cut:

- 1 (94"-long) piece. From piece, cut 4
(6½"-wide) **lengthwise** strips. From
strips, cut 2 (6½" × 94") side borders
and 2 (6½" × 81") top and bottom
borders.

Fan Blade Cutting Diagram

- 16 (2¾"-wide) strips. From strips, cut
31 (2¾" × 14½") sashing strips.
- 5 (2½"-wide) strips. From strips, cut
80 Fan Centers.
- 400" of 2¼"-wide bias strips. Join
strips to make bias binding.

From cream solid, cut:

- 10 (14½"-wide) strips. From strips, cut
20 (14½") background squares.
- 1 (2¾"-wide) strip. From strip, cut
12 (2¾") sashing squares.
- 4 (2¼"-wide) strips. Piece strips to make
2 (2¼" × 79½") side inner borders.

Block Assembly

1. Fold 1 Fan Blade in half lengthwise,
right sides facing. Stitch as shown in
Stitching Diagram. Trim corner.
2. Open seam and turn point right side
out. Press, centering seam as shown
in *Fan Blade Diagram.* Make 400 Fan

Stitching Diagram   **Fan Blade Diagram**

Blades.
3. Join 5 Fan Blades as shown in *Fan
Assembly Diagram.* Press seams open,

Fan Assembly Diagram

being careful not to stretch fabric.
Make 4 fans.
4. Pin 1 pieced fan on 1 cream background square, aligning outside raw
edges of fan with sides of square as
shown in *Block Assembly Diagram* on

Block Assembly Diagram

5. Appliqué fan points on background square. Turn under curved edge of center and appliqué on fan.

6. Trim background fabric from behind Fan Blades and Fan Center, leaving ¼" seam allowances. Trim excess Fan Blade fabric from behind fan tips, being careful not to cut top fabric.

7. Repeat for remaining 4 corners to complete 1 Fan block (*Block Diagram*). Make 20 blocks.

Block Diagram

Quilt Assembly

1. Lay out blocks, sashing strips and sashing squares as shown in the *Quilt Top Assembly Diagram*. Join into rows; join rows to complete quilt center.

2. Add cream borders to sides of quilt center.

3. Add blue borders to quilt, mitering corners.

Sew Smart™

Instructions for mitering borders can be downloaded at FonsandPorter.com/mborders. —Marianne

Finishing

1. Divide backing fabric into 3 (2½-yard) lengths. Join panels lengthwise. Seams will run horizontally.

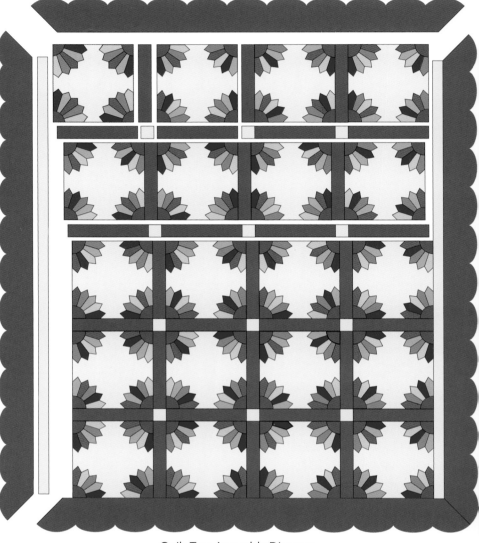

Quilt Top Assembly Diagram

2. Layer backing, batting, and quilt top; baste.

3. Using tailor's chalk, draw a gentle curved line along edge of blue border.

4. Quilt as desired. Quilt shown was quilted with a medallion design in the block centers, was outline quilted in Fan Blades, and has a diamond grid in the sashing and a cable in the outer border (*Quilting Diagram*).

5. Stitch binding to quilt along marked line. Trim quilt about ⅜" outside stitched line. Turn binding to back, and whipstitch in place.

Quilting Diagram

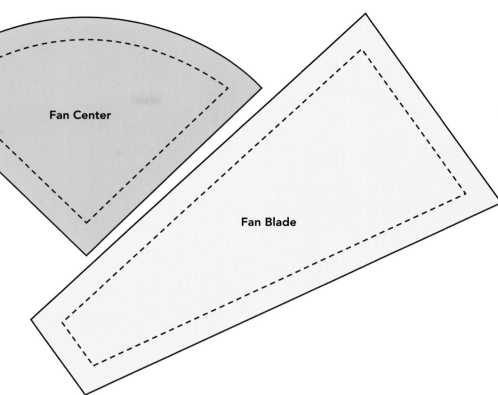

Fan Center

Fan Blade

AUTHOR

Mary Koval has been a collector and dealer of antique quilts and fabric for over 30 years. She sells her quilts at major shows in the United States and travels to lecture in Asia and Europe. As an antique quilt expert, Mary designs reproduction fabrics for Windham Fabrics and has authored three books about antique quilts. ✳

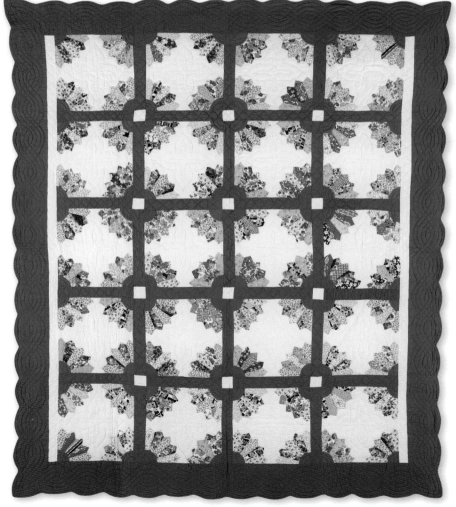

QUILT DESIGNED BY **Vicki Lynn Oehlke**.
MADE BY **Kim Kenner**. MACHINE QUILTED BY **Barb Simons**.

Baskets in the Garden

Blooming with 1930s prints, this scrappy basket
quilt features dimensional appliqué and a unique border
corner treatment.

PROJECT RATING: INTERMEDIATE
Size: 86½" × 100¾"
Blocks: 20 (10") Basket blocks

MATERIALS

NOTE: The buttons on this quilt may present a choking hazard for small children.

5 yards cream solid for block backgrounds and inner border

4½ yards blue print for outer border and binding

1⅛ yards yellow print for corner baskets and middle border

10 fat quarters★ assorted 1930s reproduction prints in red, yellow, green, blue, lavender, and pink for baskets

3 fat quarters★ assorted green 1930s reproduction prints for leaves

3 fat quarters★ assorted red 1930s reproduction prints for flowers

2 fat quarters★ assorted yellow 1930s reproduction prints for flowers

Paper-backed fusible web

27 (⅝"–diameter) assorted red and white buttons

7½ yards backing fabric

Queen-size quilt batting

★fat quarter = 18" × 20"

Cutting

Patterns for Petals and Leaves are on page 41. Follow manufacturer's instructions for using fusible web. Measurements include ¼" seam allowances. Border strips are exact length needed. You may want to make them longer to allow for piecing variations.

From cream solid, cut:

- 2 (15⅜"-wide) strips. From strips, cut 4 (15⅜") squares. Cut squares in half diagonally in both directions to make 16 side setting triangles (2 are extra).
- 1 (10⅞"-wide) strip. From strip, cut 3 (10⅞") squares. Cut squares in half diagonally to make 6 half-square C triangles (1 is extra).
- 4 (10½"-wide) strips. From strips, cut 12 (10½") setting squares.
- 1 (8⅜"-wide) strip. From strip, cut 2 (8⅜") squares. Cut squares in half diagonally to make 4 G triangles.
- 1 (8"-wide) strip. From strip, cut 2 (8") squares. Cut squares in half diagonally to make 4 corner setting triangles.
- 9 (2⅞"-wide) strips. From strips, cut 111 (2⅞") squares. Cut squares in half diagonally to make 222 half-square A triangles (1 is extra).
- 16 (2½"-wide) strips. Piece strips to make 2 (2½" × 71¼") side inner borders and 2 (2½" × 57") top and bottom inner borders. From remaining strips, cut 40 (2½" × 6½") E rectangles and 34 (2½") D squares.

From blue print, cut:

- 9 (11½"-wide) strips. Piece strips to make 2 (11½" × 71¼") side outer borders and 2 (11½" × 57") top and bottom outer borders.
- 1 (8⅜"-wide) strip. From strip, cut 4 (8⅜") squares. Cut squares in half diagonally to make 4 half-square G triangles.
- 4 (4½"-wide) strips. From strips, cut 4 (4½" × 24") J rectangles.
- 10 (2¼"-wide) strips for binding.

From yellow print, cut:

- 1 (8⅜"-wide) strip. From strip, cut 2 (8⅜") squares. Cut squares in half diagonally to make 4 half-square G triangles.

- 1 (3⅞"-wide) strip. From strip, cut 4 (3⅞") squares. Cut squares in half diagonally to make 8 half-square H triangles.
- 8 (2½"-wide) strips. Piece strips to make 2 (2½" × 71¼") side middle borders and 2 (2½" × 57") top and bottom middle borders.

From each assorted print fat quarter, cut:

- 1 (6⅞"-wide) strip. From strip, cut 1 (6⅞") square. Cut square in half diagonally to make 2 half-square B triangles.
- 1 (3⅛"-wide) strip. From strip, cut 3 (3⅛") squares. Cut squares in half diagonally to make 6 half-square I triangles.
- 2 (2⅞"-wide) strips. From strips, cut 9 (2⅞") squares. Cut squares in half diagonally to make 18 half-square A triangles.

From each green fat quarter, cut:

- 12 (2" × 3") rectangles for Large Leaves.
- 18 (2" × 2½") rectangles for Medium Leaves.
- 12 (1½" × 2") rectangles for Small Leaves.

From red fat quarters, cut a total of:

- 10 sets of 2 matching 3" squares for Large Petals.
- 16 sets of 2 matching 2¾" squares for Medium Petals.
- 8 sets of 2 matching 2¼" squares for Small Petals.

From yellow fat quarters, cut a total of:

- 8 sets of 2 matching 3" squares for Large Petals.
- 2 sets of 2 matching 2¾" squares for Medium Petals.
- 10 sets of 2 matching 2¼" squares for Small Petals.

Pieced Block Assembly

1. Join 1 print A triangle and 1 cream A triangle as shown in *Triangle-Square Diagrams*. Make 176 triangle-squares.

Triangle-Square Diagrams

2. Lay out 10 assorted triangle-squares, 3 cream A triangles, 1 cream D square, 2 cream E rectangles, and 1 set of 2 matching triangle-squares and 1 B triangle as shown in *Basket Block 1 Assembly Diagram*. Join into sections; join sections to complete 1 Basket block 1 (*Basket Block 1 Diagram*). Make 8 Basket block 1.

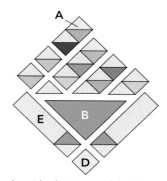

Basket Block 1 Assembly Diagram

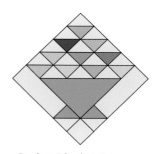

Basket Block 1 Diagram

3. Lay out 8 assorted triangle-squares, 3 cream A triangles, 3 cream D squares, 2 cream E rectangles, and 1 set of 2 matching triangle-squares and 1 B triangle as shown in *Basket Block 2 Assembly Diagram*. Join into sections; join sections to complete 1 Basket block 2 (*Basket Block 2 Diagram*). Make 7 Basket block 2.

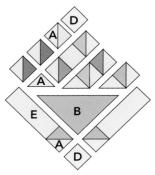

Basket Block 2 Assembly Diagram

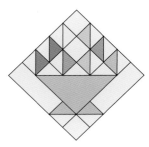

Basket Block 2 Diagram

Flower Basket Block Assembly

1. Referring to *Petal Unit Assembly Diagrams,* select 1 set of 2 matching yellow 2¼" squares. Trace Small Petal pattern onto wrong side of 1 square. Place marked square atop matching square, right sides facing. Stitch on traced line through both layers. Trim away excess fabric, leaving a scant ¼" seam allowance. Clip curves and points. Make a small slit in the center of one petal piece. Turn right side out through slit; press. Whipstitch opening closed to complete 1 Small Petal Unit. Make 10 yellow Small Petal Units and 8 red Small Petal Units.

Petal Unit Assembly Diagrams

2. In the same manner make 16 red Medium Petal Units, 2 yellow Medium Petal Units, 10 red Large Petal Units, and 8 yellow Large Petal Units.

3. Select 1 set of 2 matching green 1½" × 2" rectangles. Trace leaf pattern onto wrong side of 1 rectangle. Place marked rectangle atop matching rectangle, right sides facing. Stitch on traced line through both layers. Trim away excess fabric, leaving a scant ¼" seam allowance. Clip curves and points. Make a small slit in the center of one leaf piece. Turn right side out through slit and press to complete 1 Small Leaf. Make 18 Small Leaves.

4. In the same manner, use 2" × 2½" green rectangles to make 27 Medium Leaves and 2" × 3" green rectangles to make 18 Large Leaves.

5. Place 2 matching I triangles right sides together and stitch on 2 short sides as shown in *Triangle Point Diagrams.* Turn right side out and press. Make 3 matching Triangle Points. Make 9 sets of 3 matching Triangle Points.

Triangle Point Diagrams

6. Lay out 1 cream D square, 2 cream E rectangles, and 1 set of 2 matching triangle-squares and 1 B triangle as shown in *Flower Basket Block Assembly Diagrams.* Join into sections; join sections. Trim E rectangles as shown to complete basket unit.

7. Select 3 matching Triangle Points. Referring to *Flower Basket Block Diagram,* align raw edges of Triangle Points with top of basket unit, overlapping as necessary. Pin or baste in place.

8. Add cream C triangle to top of basket unit, catching triangle points in seam.

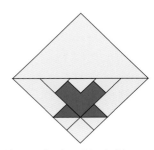

Flower Basket Block Diagram

Corner Basket Assembly

1. Select 3 matching Triangle Points, 1 yellow G triangle, 1 cream G triangle, 2 blue G triangles, and 2 yellow H triangles. Align blue G triangles, wrong sides facing; place ruler atop triangles with 5" line along left edge as shown in *Cutting Diagram.* Trim off right corner of triangles.

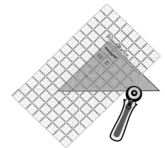

Cutting Diagram

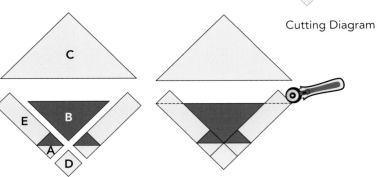

Flower Basket Block Assembly Diagrams

2. Referring to *Corner Unit Diagrams*, join 1 trimmed blue G piece and 1 yellow H triangle to complete Unit 1. Make 4 Unit 1. In the same manner, make 4 Unit 2.

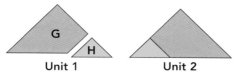

Corner Unit Diagrams

3. Join 1 Unit 1 and 1 Unit 2 to yellow G triangle as shown in *Corner Basket Assembly Diagram*.

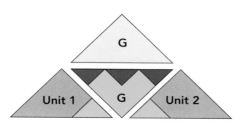

Corner Basket Assembly Diagram

4. Align raw edges of Triangle Points with top of yellow G triangle, spacing evenly. Pin or baste in place.

5. Add cream G triangle to yellow G triangle, catching Triangle Points in seam to complete Corner Basket (*Corner Basket Diagram*).

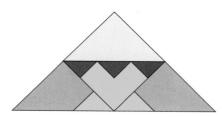

Corner Basket Diagram

Quilt Assembly

1. Lay out blocks, setting squares, and setting triangles as shown in *Quilt Top Assembly Diagram*.

2. Join into diagonal rows; join rows to complete quilt center.

3. Referring to *Quilt Top Assembly Diagram*, join cream, yellow, and blue side border strips as shown. Add borders to quilt center.

4. In the same manner, join cream, yellow, and blue top and bottom border strips as shown. Add 1 Corner Basket to each end of pieced borders. Add borders to quilt.

5. Add 1 blue J rectangle to each corner. Trim J rectangles as shown.

Finishing

1. Divide backing fabric into 3 (2½-yard) lengths. Join panels lengthwise. Seams will run horizontally.

2. Layer backing, batting, and quilt top; baste. Quilt as desired. Quilt shown was outline quilted in basket triangles, has an overall design in the background and outer border, and has curved double lines in the yellow border (*Quilting Diagram*).

3. Pair 1 small or medium petal unit with 1 medium or large petal unit. Center a button on pair and stitch through all layers to complete 1 flower unit.

4. Arrange 7 assorted leaves and 3 flower units on each Flower Basket block background and each Corner Basket as shown in *Quilt Top Assembly Diagram* and photo on page 40. Appliqué leaves in place. Tack petal units to quilt at each inner point of large petal.

5. Join 2¼"-wide blue print strips into 1 continuous piece for straight-grain French-fold binding. Add binding to quilt.

Quilting Diagram

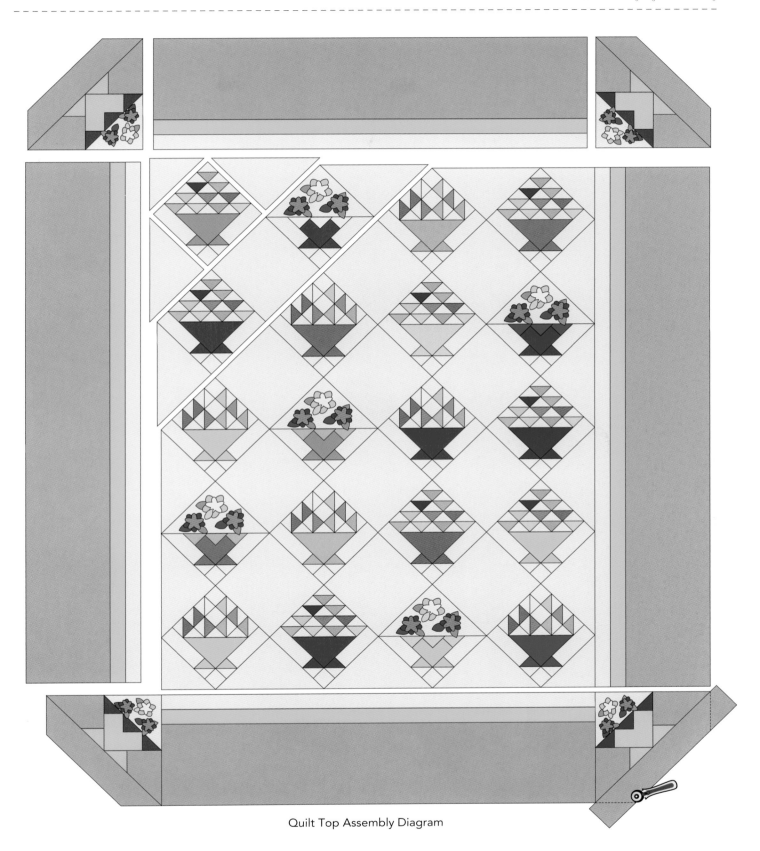

Quilt Top Assembly Diagram

Medium Leaf

Large Petal

Small Petal

Large Leaf

Medium Petal

Small leaf

DESIGNERS

Designers Vicki Lynn Oehlke and Sonja Moen formed *WillowBerry Lane* six years ago. Their business is located in a 1920s Arts and Crafts bungalow in Devils Lake, North Dakota. Together, Vicki and Sonja have published seven books. ✳

Daisy Dance

Kathy Munkelwitz hand appliquéd and hand quilted this classic quilt using prints from her collection of feed sack fabrics.

PROJECT RATING: INTERMEDIATE

Size: 80" × 97"

Blocks: 20 (12") Daisy Dance blocks

MATERIALS

4 fat quarters★ assorted green 1930s reproduction prints

12 fat quarters★ assorted 1930s reproduction prints in blue, red, pink, and yellow

7½ yards white solid for background

¼ yard green solid for stems

1¼ yards blue print for inner border and binding

9 yards backing fabric

Paper-backed fusible web

Green perle cotton

Fons & Porter Quarter Inch Seam Marker (optional)

Queen-size quilt batting

★fat quarter = 18" × 20"

Cutting

Measurements include ¼" seam allowances. Border strips are exact length needed. You may want to make them longer to allow for piecing variations. Patterns for appliqué are on page 46. Follow manufacturer's instructions for using fusible web. Instructions are written for using the Fons & Porter Quarter Inch Seam Marker. If not using the Quarter Inch Seam Marker, follow Cutting NOTES.

From green fat quarters, cut:

• 40 Leaves.

• 40 Leaves reversed.

From remaining assorted fat quarters, cut:

• 240 (2⅜") squares.

  NOTE: If not using Fons & Porter Quarter Inch Seam Marker, cut squares in half diagonally to make 480 half-square D triangles.

• 60 sets of 5 matching Petals.

• 60 Flower Centers.

From white solid, cut:

- 2 (14"-wide) strips. From strips, cut 4 (14") squares. Cut squares in half diagonally in both directions to make 16 quarter-square E triangles (2 are extra).
- 7 (12½"-wide) strips. From strips, cut 20 (12½") A squares.
- 3 (9½"-wide) strips. From strips, cut 12 (9½") B squares.
- 1 (7¼"-wide) strip. From strip, cut 2 (7¼") squares. Cut squares in half diagonally to make 4 half-square F triangles.
- 10 (5"-wide) strips. Piece strips to make 2 (5" × 88½") side outer borders and 2 (5" × 80½") top and bottom outer borders
- 17 (2⅜"-wide) strips. From strips, cut 258 (2⅜") squares. Cut 18 squares in half diagonally to make 36 half-square D triangles. Use remaining squares to make half-square triangle units.

  NOTE: If not using Fons & Porter Quarter Inch Seam Marker, cut all squares in half diagonally to make 516 half-square D triangles.

- 4 (2"-wide) strips. From strips, cut 62 (2") C squares.

From green solid, cut:

- 60 (¾" × 4") bias strips for stems. Fold bias strips in thirds, press, and hand baste fold in place to prepare stems for appliqué.

From blue print, cut:

- 10 (2¼"-wide) strips for binding.
- 9 (2"-wide) strips. Piece strips to make 2 (2" × 85½") side inner borders and 2 (2" × 71½") top and bottom inner borders.

Daisy Block Assembly

1. Choose 3 sets of 5 matching Petals, 3 Flower Centers, 2 Leaves, 2 Leaves reversed, and 3 stems.
2. Referring to *Daisy Block Diagram* for placement, lay out pieces on 1 white solid A square.

Daisy Block Diagram

3. Appliqué pieces on background.
4. Using green pearl cotton, stitch stems with chain stitch, leaf veins with stem stitch, and tendrils with straight stitch as shown in photo on page 43 (*Chain Stitch, Stem Stitch, Straight Stitch Diagrams*).

Chain Stitch Diagram

Stem Stitch Diagram

Straight Stitch Diagram

5. Make 20 blocks.

NOTE: 10 blocks have stems curving to left and 10 blocks have stems curving to right.

Pieced Block Assembly

1. Place 1 white (2⅜") square atop 1 print (2⅜") square, right sides facing. Place Fons & Porter Quarter Inch Seam Marker diagonally across the square, with the yellow center line positioned exactly at opposite corners. Mark stitching lines along both sides of the Quarter Inch Seam Marker. Stitch along both marked sewing lines. Cut between rows of stitching to make 2 triangle-squares (*Triangle-Square Diagrams*). Repeat to make 480 triangle-squares.

NOTE: If not using Fons & Porter Quarter Inch Seam Marker, join 1 white D triangle and 1 print D triangle to make a triangle-square. Make 480 triangle-squares.

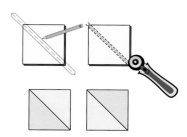

Triangle-Square Diagrams

2. Join 6 assorted triangle-squares as shown in *Side Unit Diagrams*. Make 80 Side Units.

Side Unit Diagrams

3. Lay out 4 Side Units, 1 white B square, and 4 white C squares as shown in *Pieced Block Assembly Diagram*. Join into rows; join rows to complete

1 Pieced block *(Pieced Block Diagram)*. Make 12 Pieced blocks.

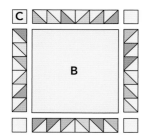

C

B

Pieced Block Assembly Diagram

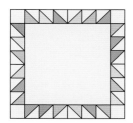

Pieced Block Diagram

Setting Triangles Assembly

1. Lay out 2 Side Units, 1 white E triangle, 1 white C square, and 2 white D triangles as shown in *Setting Triangle Assembly Diagram.* Join to complete 1 Setting Triangle. *(Setting Triangle Diagram).* Make 14 Setting Triangles.

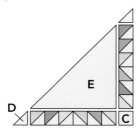

E

D   C

Setting Triangle Assembly Diagram

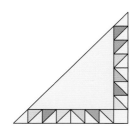

Setting Triangle Diagram

2. Lay out 1 Side Unit, 1 white F triangle, and 2 white D triangles as shown in *Corner Triangle Assembly Diagram.* Join to complete 1 Corner Triangle *(Corner Triangle Diagram).* Make 4 Corner Triangles.

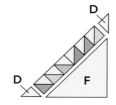

D

D   F

Corner Triangle Assembly Diagram

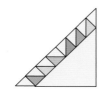

Corner Triangle Diagram

Quilt Assembly

1. Lay out blocks, setting triangles, and corner triangles as shown in *Quilt Top Assembly Diagram* on page 46. Join into diagonal rows; join rows to complete quilt center.

2. Add blue print side inner borders to quilt center. Add top and bottom inner borders to quilt.

3. Repeat for white outer borders.

Finishing

1. Divide backing into 3 (3-yard) lengths. Join panels lengthwise. Seams will run horizontally.

2. Layer backing, batting, and quilt top; baste. Quilt as desired. Quilt shown was outline quilted around appliqué and half-square triangle units, has a leaf design in pieced blocks, setting triangles, and borders, and ½" grid in background areas *(Quilting Diagram).*

3. Join 2¼"-wide blue print strips into 1 continuous piece for straight-grain French-fold binding. Add binding to quilt.

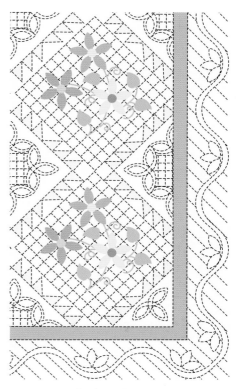

Quilting Diagram

Quilt Top Assembly Diagram

Petal

Flower Center

Leaf

Patterns are shown full size for use wi
fusible web. Add ³⁄₁₆" seam allowan
for hand appliqué

WEB EXTRA
Go to www.FonsandPorter.com/
daisysizes to download *Quilt Top
Assembly Diagrams* for these size
options.

SIZE OPTIONS

	Throw (46" × 63")	Twin (63" × 97")	King (114" × 114")
Daisy Blocks	6	15	36
Pieced Blocks	2	8	25

MATERIALS

Green Prints	2 fat quarters	3 fat quarters	8 fat quarters
Assorted Prints	4 fat quarters	9 fat quarters	22 fat quarters
White Solid	2¾ yards	5 yards	12 yards
Green Solid	¼ yard	¼ yard	½ yard
Blue Print	1 yard	1¼ yards	1⅝ yards
Backing Fabric	3 yards	6 yards	10¼ yards
Batting	Twin-size	Queen-size	King-size

DESIGNER

Professional quiltmaker Kathy Munkelwitz has won many national awards. She lives in Minnesota, where she loves to hunt and fish. Kathy is the mother of three daughters, a grandmother, and now a great-grandmother—and she still finds time to quilt! ✳

QUILT DESIGNED BY **John Flynn**.
MADE BY **Diane Ide**. MACHINE QUILTED BY **Dawn Cavanaugh**.

Double Wedding Ring

Make this traditional quilt in assorted batiks for a contemporary twist. To cut your fabric pieces, use our patterns for templates or purchase a set of rotary cutting templates. See the *Sew Easy* lessons on pages 52 and 54 for tips on piecing the quilt and attaching the binding.

PROJECT RATING: CHALLENGING
Size: 92⅝" × 105"
Blocks: 56 (18") rings

MATERIALS

NOTE: Fabrics in the quilt shown are from SewBatik™.

½ yard each of 26 assorted bright batiks for rings

6½ yards tan batik for background

⅞ yard blue print batik for binding

Template material

8¼ yards backing fabric

King-size quilt batting

Cutting

Patterns for templates are on page 55. Measurements include ¼" seam allowances.

From each bright batik, cut:

• 40 A.
• 10 B.
• 10 B reversed.
• 10 C.

From tan batik, cut:

• 127 D.
• 56 E.

From blue print batik, cut:

• 2"-wide bias strips. Join to make about 450" of bias for binding.

Block Assembly

NOTE: Refer to *Sew Easy: Piecing Double Wedding Ring* on page 52 for detailed instructions, step-by-step photos, and sewing tips.

1. Referring to *Melon Unit Assembly* on page 52, join pieces to make 1 Melon Unit (*Melon Unit Diagrams*). Make 127 Melon Units.

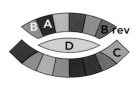

Melon Unit Diagrams

2. Referring to *Block Unit Diagrams* and *Block Unit Assembly* on page 53, join 2 Melon Unit to 1 E piece to complete 1 Block Unit. Make 56 Block Units.

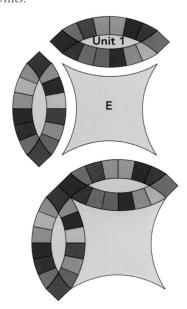

Block Unit Diagrams

Quilt Assembly

1. Lay out Melon and Block Units as shown in *Quilt Top Assembly Diagram*.

2. Referring to *Quilt Assembly* in *Sew Easy: Piecing Double Wedding Ring* on page 53, join units into rows. Join rows.

Finishing

1. Divide backing fabric into 3 (2¾-yard) pieces. Join panels lengthwise; seams will run horizontally.

2. Layer backing, batting, and quilt top; baste. Quilt as desired. Quilt shown was quilted in the ditch in the rings and with feather designs in the background. (Feather motifs designed by Dawn Cavanaugh are given as dashed lines on template patterns on page 55.)

3. Referring to *Sew Easy: Binding Uneven Edges* on page 54, add binding to quilt.

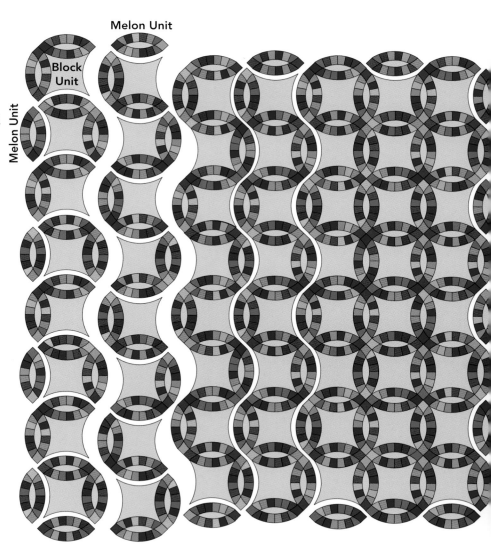

Quilt Top Assembly Diagram

We have included several variations to show possible color arrangements. ✳

Melon Unit

Make just three rings for a table runner.

To make the 1930s version pictured, you'll need 1 yard of background fabric plus scraps of assorted prints and two solids. You'll also need batting and fabric for backing and binding.

Cutting

From background fabric, cut:

3 E.

10 D.

From assorted prints, cut:

80 A.

20 B.

20 B reversed.

From each of 2 solids, cut:

10 C.

BY **John Flynn**.

Sew Easy™

Piecing Double Wedding Ring

Piecing a Double Wedding Ring quilt is easier than it first appears, once you know a few tricks. You'll find the quilt goes together smoothly as you get more practice at managing the curved seams and matching the critical points.

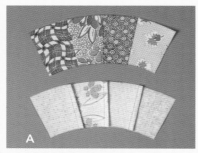

A

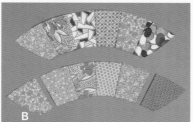

B

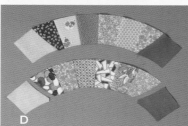

C

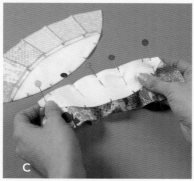

D

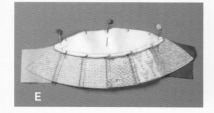

E

Melon Unit Assembly

1. Join 4 A wedges (*Photo A*).
2. Add B piece to 1 end of arc and B reverse piece to opposite end to complete 1 arc (*Photo B*). Make 2 arcs. With arc right side up, press seam allowances to the left.
3. Pin D melon to arc, matching ends and center, adding additional pins as desired (*Photo C*). With the melon on top, stitch melon to arc. Press seam allowances toward arc.
4. Add 1 C corner piece to each end of remaining arc (*Photo D*). (If you are using 2 colors for corner pieces, add a different colored C piece to each end.) Press seams toward corner pieces.
5. Working with the melon on top, pin intersections where C corner pieces meet adjacent arc (*Photo E*). Align edges of B and C pieces; stitch to first corner intersection, stopping with needle in fabric (*Photo F*). Lift presser foot and adjust fabric, aligning edge of melon to arc. Stitch to other corner intersection, stop with needle down, raise presser foot, align edges, and finish seam to complete Melon Unit.

F

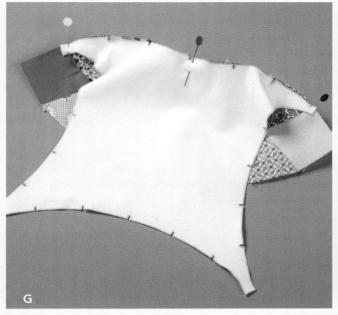

Block Unit Assembly

The basic piecing Unit for a Double Wedding Ring quilt is a center piece with Melon Units added to adjacent sides.

1. Working with the center piece on top, pin 1 Melon Unit to top edge of center piece. Pin at center and ¼" from ends (*Photo G*).

2. Sew in at a 45-degree angle to the first pin, stop with needle down, raise presser foot, pivot, and sew along curved edge to the opposite end pin. Stop and pivot as before (*Photo H*) and sew off the end at a 45-degree angle. The angled beginning and ends of seams (*Photo I*) will allow you to chain piece as you assemble units. **Do not press seams until second Melon Unit has been added.**

3. With center piece on top, pin second Melon Unit to left edge of center piece, matching intersections of C corner pieces. Holding seam allowance of bottom C piece out of the way, stitch to intersection, backstitch, and remove

from machine. Align edge of center piece with melon. Stitch in from corner at 45-degree angle. With needle down, stop at intersection, lift presser foot, and adjust fabric. Stitch curved seam. At the end corner intersection, pivot and sew off the corner at an angle (*Photo J*). Press seams toward arcs.

Sew **Smart**™

If you are using two colors for contrasting C corners, you will need to make an equal number of two slightly different block units (Block X and Block Y) with opposite color placement of the corner C pieces (*Photo K*). —John

Quilt Assembly

1. Lay out Block Units in rows. (If you are using contrasting corners, alternate the two types of blocks in each row.)

2. Join Block Units into rows. Join rows. Add Melon Units to fill in outer edge of quilt.

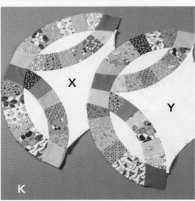

Binding Uneven Edges

Use this technique to bind a quilt that has inside corners or scalloped edges.

1. Trim batting and backing even with quilt top. At inside corners, clip almost to a quarter inch from edge (*Photo A*).

> ## Sew **Smart**™
>
> If your quilting does not go all the way to the edge of the quilt, use a walking foot to baste the layers together about ⅛" from the edge before trimming the quilt. —Marianne

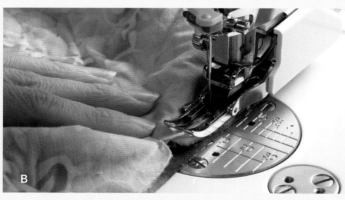
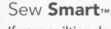

2. With binding on bottom and quilt back side up, use a walking foot to stitch binding to quilt ¼" from edge. At inside corners, pull on clipped area to straighten the quilt (*Photo B*). Be sure stitching clears the clipped area.
3. Fold binding to back of quilt. At the inside corners, fold the binding to create a miter (*Photo C*). Hand stitch binding to quilt back, stitching mitered fold at inside corners.

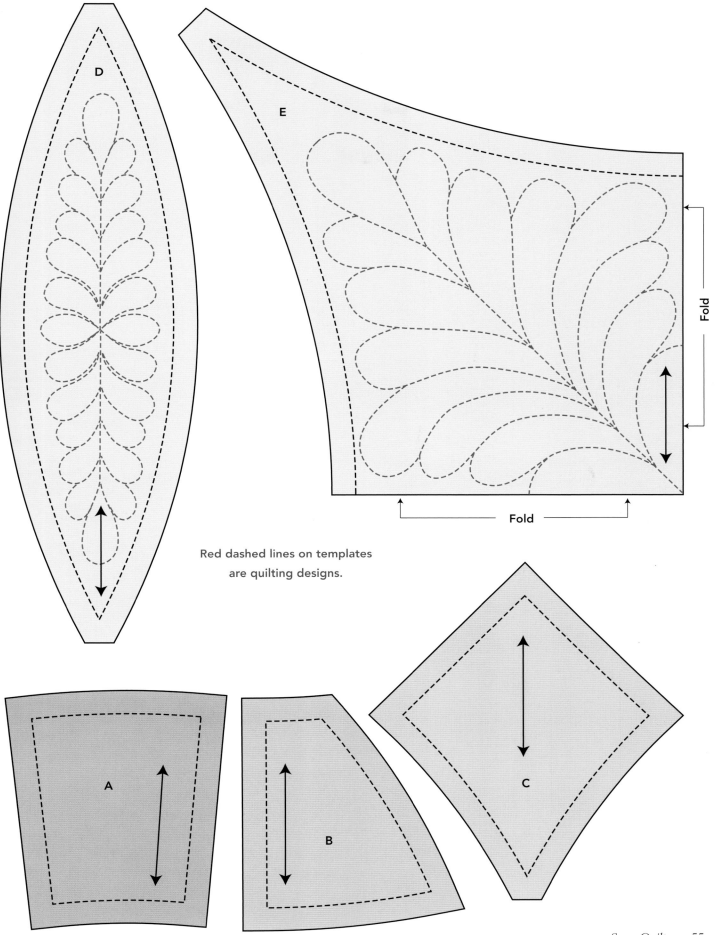

Red dashed lines on templates
are quilting designs.

Circle Jubilee

Inspired by an antique appliqué design, Pam Clarke created this charming quilt to use up some of her scraps. See *Sew Easy: Making Perfect Circles* on page 61 for Pam's easy appliqué method.

PROJECT RATING: INTERMEDIATE

Size: 95" × 95"

Blocks: 16 (19") Circle Jubilee blocks

MATERIALS

25 fat quarters★ assorted prints for circles

2½ yards green print for stems and leaves

7½ yards cream print for background

¾ yard burgundy print for binding

8⅝ yards backing fabric

Freezer paper

Temporary basting spray

King-size quilt batting

★fat quarter = 18" × 20"

Cutting

Patterns for appliqué shapes are on pages 58 and 59. Measurements include ¼" seam allowances.

From each fat quarter, cut:

Refer to *Sew Easy: Making Perfect Circles* on page 61 for instructions on cutting the circles for this quilt.

• 1 Large Circle.

• 28 Small Circles. (You will have a few extra.)

From green print, cut:

• 12 (1¼"-wide) strips for stems.

• 400 Leaves.

Use Pam Clarke's method shown in *Sew Easy: Making Perfect Circles* on page 61 to cut Leaves.

From cream print, cut:

• 8 (19½"-wide) strips. From strips, cut 16 (19½") squares.

• 9 (10"-wide) strips. From strips, cut 16 (10" × 19½") rectangles and 4 (10") squares.

From burgundy print, cut:

• 10 (2¼"-wide) strips for binding.

Block Assembly

1. Fold 1 (1¼"-wide) green print strip in half lengthwise, wrong sides together; stitch along raw edges using ¼" seam allowance. Finger press seam allowance open down the center of the back of the strip; press. From stitched strip, cut 9 (4¼"-long) stems. Make 100 stems.

2. Referring to *Sew Easy: Making Perfect Circles* on page 61, prepare small and large circles for appliqué. Set aside large circles to add to quilt top after blocks are sewn together.

3. Referring to *Block Diagram*, lay out pieces as shown. Appliqué stems, leaves, and small circles on background. Make 16 blocks.

Block Diagram

4. In a similar manner, make 19 half blocks (*Half Block Diagram*) and 4 corner blocks (*Corner Block Diagram*).

Half Block Diagram

Corner Block Diagram

Quilt Assembly

1. Lay out blocks as shown in *Quilt Top Assembly Diagram*. Join blocks into rows; join rows.

2. As you join rows, appliqué large circles over intersections of blocks.

Finishing

1. Divide backing fabric into 3 (2⅞-yard) pieces. Join panels lengthwise. Seams will run horizontally.

2. Layer backing, batting, and quilt top; baste. Quilt as desired. Quilt shown was quilted with floral designs and an overall small meandering pattern in background (*Quilting Diagram*).

3. Join 2¼"-wide burgundy print strips into 1 continuous piece for straight-grain French-fold binding. Add binding to quilt.

Quilt Top Assembly Diagram

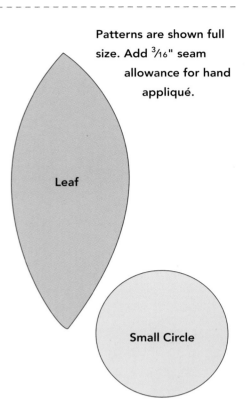

Patterns are shown full size. Add ³⁄₁₆" seam allowance for hand appliqué.

Leaf

Small Circle

Quilting Diagram

TRIED & TRUE

For a different look, we used only red prints for the circles. Fabrics shown are from the Madeline collection by Janet Orfini for Lyndhurst Studio.

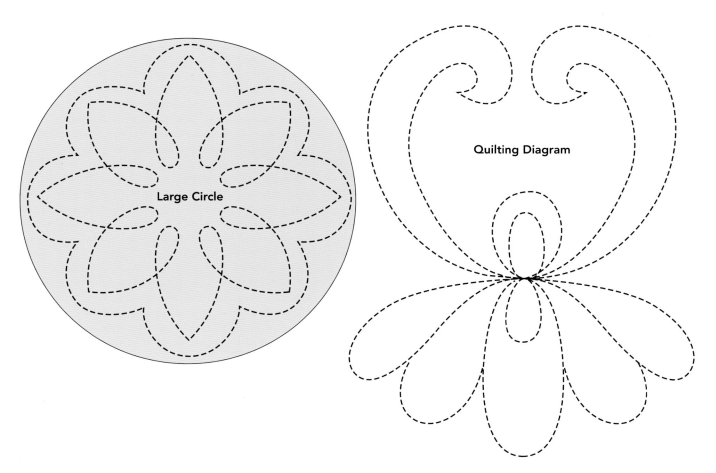

Large Circle

Quilting Diagram

DESIGNER

Pam Clarke started making quilts in the early 1970s, and is now a longarm quilting instructor. She is known for her machine quilting technique, Designs with Lines. This method speeds up the quilting process by using registration marks combined with simple lines. Her favorite type of quilts is scrap quilts that incorporate appliqué. ✳

BY **Pam Clarke.**

Making Perfect Circles

Whether you machine or hand appliqué, using a circle cutter and basting spray makes easy work of cutting and appliquéing multiple identical pieces.

1. Fold a large piece of freezer paper (at least 24" long) accordion style to make four layers. Staple layers together to prevent shifting when cutting.

2. Using scissors or a circle cutter adjusted to cut desired size, cut through all four layers of paper to make multiple circle templates *(Photo A)*.

3. Iron circle paper templates onto wrong side of fabric, leaving at least ½" between each piece for seam allowances. With scissors, cut around each template, leaving a scant ¼" seam allowance to fold under *(Photo B)*.

4. Lay pieces face down on newspaper or inside a shallow box and spray lightly with temporary basting spray.

5. Finger press seam allowance to back of template *(Photo C)*. Do not clip seam allowance. The basting spray will hold the edges in place for several days, longer if kept in a sealed bag or container.

6. Appliqué circles in place using a traditional hand method or machine appliqué with a narrow zigzag or blanket stitch.

Sew **Smart**™

When machine stitching, use a clear thread on top so that your stitching does not show. —Pam

7. Cut away background fabric approximately ¼" inside the stitching *(Photo D)*. Remove paper templates. To make removal easy, use your iron to gently warm the freezer paper and reactivate the basting spray.

Sew **Smart**™

Use bamboo skewers to pick up the sprayed pieces and to help tuck under the edges while sewing. —Pam

A

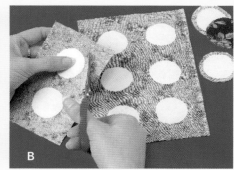

B

C

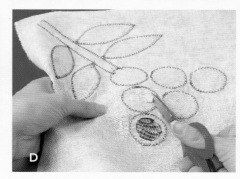

D

Lotsa Potsa Flowers

This signature quilt designed by Betsy DeFazio was a gift for her guild's outgoing president. Large, "fussy-cut" flower motifs transform Snowball blocks into potted plants, each signed by a member of the group.

PROJECT RATING: INTERMEDIATE
Size: 71" × 77"
Blocks: 24 (14" × 10") Flowerpot blocks

MATERIALS

72 (4½") A squares "fussy cut" from assorted floral prints for flowers

72 (4½" × 3½") B rectangles in assorted pastels for flowerpots

1⅛ yards or 24 (1½" × 40") strips cream/beige prints for background

¼ yard green print for stems

1 yard light brown print for window sashing strips

¾ yard medium brown print for window sashing strips

1 yard beige print for sashing

1⅞ yards dark brown print for border and binding

4¾ yards backing fabric

Full-size quilt batting

Cutting

Measurements include ¼" seam allowances. Border strips are exact length needed. You may want to make them longer to allow for piecing variations.

From each cream/beige strip, cut:

• 6 (1½" × 2") D rectangles.

• 18 (1½") C squares.

From green print, cut:

• 3 (1½"-wide) strips. From strips, cut 72 (1½") C squares.

From light brown print, cut:

• 12 (2½"-wide) strips. From strips, cut 24 (2½" × 14⅞") E rectangles. Referring to *Window Sashing Strip Diagrams*, with fabric right side up, trim left end of each rectangle at a 45–degree angle.

Window Sashing Strip Diagrams

From medium brown print, cut:

- 8 (2½"-wide) strips. From strips, cut 24 (2½" × 10⅞") F rectangles. Referring to *Window Sashing Strip Diagrams,* with fabric right side up, trim right end of each rectangle at a 45-degree angle.

From beige print, cut:

- 21 (1½"-wide) strips. From strips, cut 30 (1½" × 10½") vertical sashing strips. Piece remaining strips to make 7 (1½" × 61½") horizontal sashing strips.

From dark brown print, cut:

- 8 (5½"-wide) strips. Piece strips to make 2 (5½" × 67½") side border strips and 2 (5½" × 71½") top and bottom border strips.
- 8 (2¼"-wide) strips for binding.

Flower Unit Assembly

1. For each Flower Unit, select 1 A square, 1 B rectangle, 1 green C square, and a matching set of 6 beige C squares and 2 D rectangles.

2. Referring to *Flower Diagrams,* place 1 beige C square atop A square, right sides facing. Stitch diagonally from corner to corner. Trim ¼" beyond stitching. Press open to reveal triangle. In the same manner, add a C square to each remaining corner.

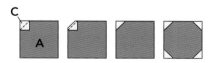

Flower Diagrams

3. Referring to *Flowerpot Diagrams,* place 1 beige print C square atop B rectangle, right sides facing. Stitch diagonally from corner to corner. Trim ¼" beyond stitching. Press open to reveal triangle. In the same manner, add a C square to adjacent corner.

Flowerpot Diagrams

4. Referring to *Flower Unit Diagrams,* lay out flower, flowerpot, 2 background D rectangles and 1 green C square. Join pieces to make 1 Flower Unit. Make 72 Flower Units.

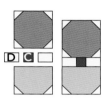

Flower Unit Diagrams

Block Assembly

1. Referring to *Block Assembly Diagram,* join 3 Flower Units. Add F window sashing piece to left side of block, stopping stitching ¼" from lower left

corner of block to allow for mitering corners. In the same manner, join E sashing piece to lower edge of block. Join angled sides of E and F pieces, beginning at inner corner and stitching to outer corner *(Block Diagram).* Make 24 Flowerpot blocks.

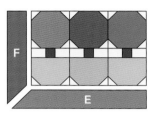

Block Assembly Diagram

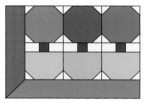

Block Diagram

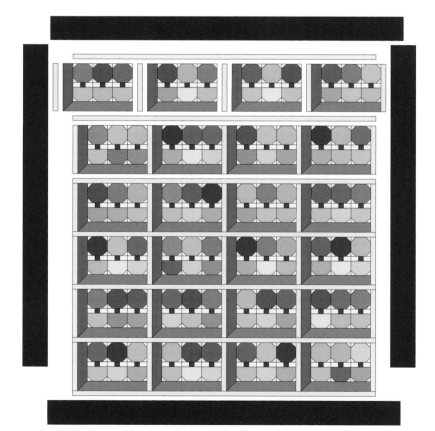

Quilt Top Assembly Diagram

Quilt Assembly

1. Lay out blocks, vertical sashing strips, and horizontal sashing strips as shown in *Quilt Top Assembly Diagram*. Join into horizontal rows; join rows to complete quilt center.

2. Add dark brown side borders to quilt center. Add dark brown top and bottom borders to quilt.

Finishing

1. Divide backing into 2 (2⅜-yard) pieces. Cut 1 piece in half lengthwise to make 2 narrow panels. Join 1 narrow panel to each side of wider panel; press seam allowances toward narrow panels.

2. Layer backing, batting, and quilt top; baste. Quilt as desired. Quilt shown was quilted in the ditch around blocks and between borders, with a flower motif in the flower patch, and straight lines in the outer border.

3. Join 2¼"-wide dark brown print strips into 1 continuous piece for straight-grain French-fold binding. Add binding to quilt.

DESIGNER

Quilter Betsy DeFazio likes to make a variety of quilts, but especially enjoys creating landscapes. When not quilting, Betsy loves to play golf. ✳

Peek-a-Boo

Create this fun quilt in a weekend for a special little one. The quilt is assembled in a few easy steps, finishing the front, back, and quilting at the same time.

PROJECT RATING: INTERMEDIATE

Size: 36" × 48"

Blocks: 48 (6") blocks

MATERIALS

24 fat eighths★ novelty prints

12 fat quarters★★ assorted bright prints in pink, red, orange, yellow, blue, green, and purple

2⅝ yards flannel for batting

Template plastic or card stock

★fat eighth = 9" × 20"

★★fat quarter = 18" × 20"

Sew **Smart**™

If you prefer to use a different novelty print in each block, you can start with 48 (9") squares to make your circles. —Liz

Cutting

Measurements include ¼" seam allowances. Make a template from the circle pattern on page 68. From template plastic or card stock, make a template for a 6" square to use to mark stitching guidelines.

From each assorted bright print, cut:

• 4 (9") squares.

From each novelty print, cut:

• 2 (9") squares, centering desired print motif in each square.

From flannel, cut

• 48 (9") squares.

Block Assembly

1. Choose 1 novelty print and 1 bright square. Place squares right sides together. Using template, draw a circle on wrong side of novelty print square, centering over print motifs as desired.

2. Pin paired squares to flannel square with wrong side of novelty print facing up so you can see the marked circle. Stitch completely around circle on drawn line through all three layers.

3. Referring to *Marking Diagram*, make a slit for turning about 3" long **only in novelty print** about ¾" from edge of drawn circle. Cut around circle ¼" outside marked line. Turn circle right side out; press. (Slit will be hidden after you join the circles.)

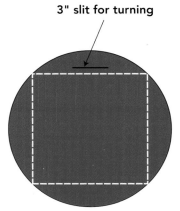

3" slit for turning

Marking Diagram

Sew **Smart**™

After stitching your circles, cut them out with pinking shears or a pinking rotary blade to make them lie flat after turning. —Liz

4. Place 6" square of card stock on novelty print side of circle and draw around square to mark stitching lines (*Marking Diagram*).

5. Repeat to make 48 circles.

Quilt Assembly

1. Lay out circles in 8 horizontal rows with 6 circles in each row.

2. Place 2 circles bright print sides facing and stitch on stitching line as shown in *Stitching Diagrams*. Continue adding circles to complete 1 row *(Row Assembly Diagram 1)*. Make 8 rows.

3. In the same manner, join rows as shown in *Row Assembly Diagram 2*.

4. Fold curved edges of circles toward center; machine blanket stitch around curves.

TIP

If you prefer, use a variety of decorative stitches and different colors of threads to stitch around the curves. —Liz

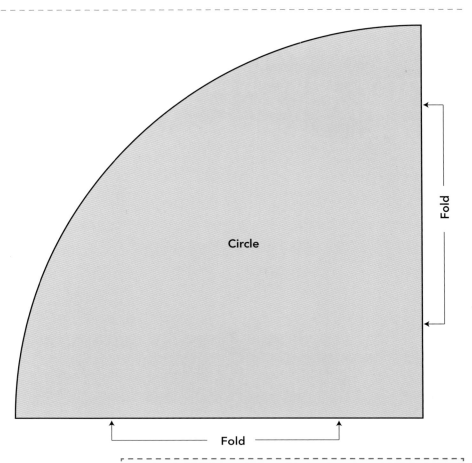

Circle

Fold

Fold

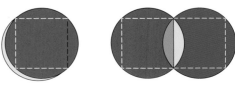

Stitching Diagrams

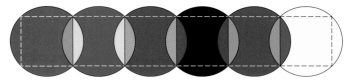

Row Assembly Diagram 1

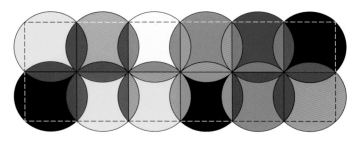

Row Assembly Diagram 2

TRIED & TRUE

For our "grown-up" version of *Peek-a-Boo*, we used a single large floral print in place of the novelty prints and a variety of coordinating prints instead of the bright prints. Fabrics shown are from the Fancy Free collection by Thimbleberries® for RJR Fabrics.

Ava Jo

A playful two-year-old toddler was the inspiration for this quick and easy baby quilt.

PROJECT RATING: EASY

Size: 37½" × 46½"

Blocks: 12 (9") blocks

MATERIALS

3 fat quarters★ assorted white prints for blocks

3 fat quarters★ assorted green prints for blocks

4 fat quarters★ assorted pink prints for blocks

⅜ yard brown print for blocks and inner border

⅝ yard pink stripe for blocks and binding

⅜ yard green print #4 for middle border

⅝ yard white print #4 for outer border

1½ yards backing fabric

Crib-size quilt batting

★fat quarter = 18" × 20"

NOTE: Fabrics in the quilt shown are from the Cozy Cotton flannel collection by Robert Kaufman Fabrics.

Cutting

Measurements include ¼" seam allowances. Border strips are exact length needed. You may want to make them longer to allow for piecing variations.

From each of 2 white print fat quarters, cut:

• 4 (2"-wide) strips for strip sets.

From remaining white print fat quarter, cut:

• 8 (1¼"-wide) strips for strip sets.

From each green print fat quarter, cut:

• 8 (1¼"-wide) strips for strip sets.

From each of 2 pink print fat quarters, cut:

• 4 (2"-wide) strips for strip sets.

From each remaining pink print fat quarter, cut:

• 8 (1¼"-wide) strips for strip sets.

From brown print, cut:

• 2 (2"-wide) strips. Cut strips in half to make 4 (2" × 20") strips for strip sets.

• 4 (1¼"-wide) strips. From strips, cut 2 (1¼" × 36½") side inner borders and 2 (1¼" × 29") top and bottom inner borders.

From pink stripe, cut:

• 5 (2½"-wide) strips for binding.

• 2 (2"-wide) strips. Cut strips in half to make 4 (2" × 20") strips for strip sets.

From green print #4, cut:

• 4 (2"-wide) strips. From strips, cut 2 (2" × 38") side middle borders and 2 (2" × 32") top and bottom middle borders.

From white print #4, cut:

• 5 (3½"-wide) strips. From strips, cut 2 (3½" × 38") top and bottom outer borders. Piece remaining strips to make 2 (3½" × 41") side outer borders.

Block A Assembly

1. Join 1 (2"-wide) brown print strip, 1 (2"-wide) pink stripe strip, and 1 (2"-wide) white print #1 strip as shown in *Strip Set #1 Diagram*. Make 4 Strip Set #1. From strip sets, cut 12 (5"-wide) #1 segments.

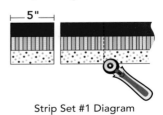

Strip Set #1 Diagram

2. Join 1 (2"-wide) white print #2 strip, 1 (2"-wide) pink print #1 strip, and 1 (2"-wide) pink print #2 strip as shown in *Strip Set #2 Diagram*. Make 4 Strip Set #2. From strip sets, cut 12 (5"-wide) #2 segments.

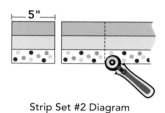

Strip Set #2 Diagram

3. Lay out 2 #1 segments and 2 #2 segments as shown in *Block A Assembly Diagram*. Join into rows; join rows to complete 1 Block A (*Block A Diagram*). Make 6 Block A.

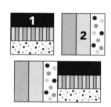

Block A Assembly Diagram

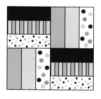

Block A Diagram

Block B Assembly

1. Join 1 (1¼"-wide) pink print #3 strip, 1 (1¼"-wide) pink print #4 strip, and 1 (1¼"-wide) white print #3 strip as shown in *Strip Set #3 Diagram*. Make 8 Strip Set #3. From strip sets, cut 48 (2¾"-wide) #3 segments.

Strip Set #3 Diagram

2. Join 1 (1¼"-wide) green print #1 strip, 1 (1¼"-wide) green print #2 strip, and 1 (1¼"-wide) green print #3 strip as shown in *Strip Set #4 Diagram*. Make 8 Strip Set #4. From strip sets, cut 48 (2¾"-wide) #4 segments.

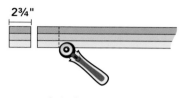

Strip Set #4 Diagram

3. Lay out 8 #3 segments and 8 #4 segments as shown in *Block B Assembly Diagram*. Join into rows; join rows to complete 1 Block B (*Block B Diagram*). Make 6 Block B.

Block B Assembly Diagram

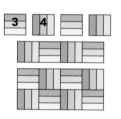

Block B Diagram

Quilt Assembly

1. Lay out blocks as shown in *Quilt Top Assembly Diagram*. Join into rows; join rows to complete quilt center.

2. Add brown print side inner borders to quilt center. Add brown print top and bottom borders to quilt.

3. Repeat for green print #4 middle borders and white print #4 outer borders.

Finishing

1. Layer backing, batting, and quilt top; baste. Quilt as desired. Quilt shown was quilted in the ditch, with a spiral pattern and diagonal grid in the blocks, and with parallel lines in the borders (*Quilting Diagram*).

2. Join 2½"-wide pink stripe strips into 1 continuous piece for straight-grain French-fold binding. Add binding to quilt.

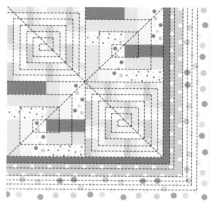

Quilting Diagram

TRIED & TRUE

We created blocks using fabrics from the versatile Dimples collection and bold prints from the Eden collection, both by Andover Fabrics.

SIZE OPTIONS

	Throw (46½" × 64½")	Twin (73½" × 91½")
Block #1	12	32
Block #2	12	31
Setting	4 × 6	7 × 9

MATERIALS

3 White Prints	⅜ yard each	¾ yard each
3 Green Prints	⅜ yard each	¾ yard each
4 Pink Prints	⅜ yard each	¾ yard each
Brown Print	½ yard	1 yard
Pink Stripe	¾ yard	1¼ yards
Green Print #4	½ yard	¾ yard
White Print #4	¾ yard	1 yard
Backing Fabric	3 yards	5½ yards
Batting	Twin-size	Full-size

WEB EXTRA

Go to www.FonsandPorter.com/avajosizes to download *Quilt Top Assembly Diagrams* for these size options.

DESIGNER

Tony Jacobson is the Art Director for *Fons & Porter's Easy Quilts*. He and his wife, Jeanne, share many of the same passions—decorating, gardening, theater, and, of course, quilting. They share their home in Winterset with two dogs, Jackson and Harley, and one cat, Barnaby Tucker.

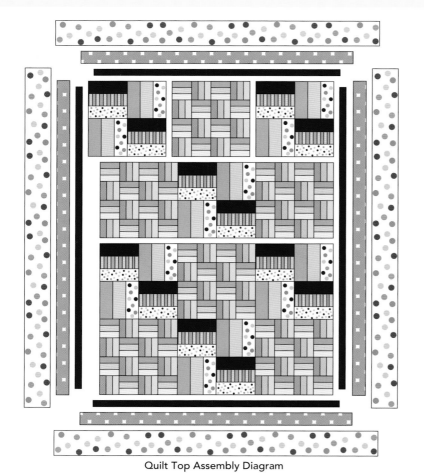

Quilt Top Assembly Diagram

QUILT BY **Kim Cairns.**
MACHINE QUILTED BY **Richard Sheldon.**

Cosmatesque

Subtle color and value differences of Daiwabo fabrics give Kim Cairns' quilt a neutral look. This quilt would be at home in any environment.

PROJECT RATING: CHALLENGING
Size: 55½" × 81"
Blocks: 23 (8") blocks

MATERIALS

NOTE: Fabrics in the quilt shown are Serenity Taupe Prints by Daiwabo for EE Schenck Fabrics.

15 fat quarters★ assorted light prints in beige, tan, and cream for blocks and border

20 fat quarters★ assorted dark prints in taupe, gray, green, and blue for setting triangles and border

¾ yard dark taupe for flange and binding

5 yards backing fabric

Twin-size quilt batting

★fat quarter = 18" × 20"

Cutting

Measurements include ¼" seam allowances.

From assorted light prints, cut a total of:
• 164 (1½"-wide) strips for strip sets.

From assorted dark prints, cut a total of:
• 198 (1½"-wide) strips for strip sets.
• 50 (1½") J squares.

From dark taupe, cut:
• 8 (2¼"-wide) strips for binding.
• 6 (1⅛"-wide) strips. From strips, cut 2 (1⅛" × 40") top and bottom flange strips. Piece remaining strips to make 2 (1⅛" × 65½") side flange strips.

Light Strip Set Assembly

1. Join 4 light print strips as shown in *Strip Set Diagram.* Make 41 light strip sets.

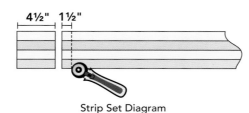

Strip Set Diagram

Sew **Smart**™
Measure the height of your strip sets. For example, a 4-strip set should measure exactly 4½". If it is not 4½", adjust seams to get the correct measurement. —Marianne

2. From strip sets, cut 92 (4½"-wide) segments and 208 (1½"-wide) segments.

Block Assembly

1. Lay out 4 (4½"-wide) light segments as shown in *Block Assembly Diagram.*

2. Join into rows; join rows to complete 1 block *(Block Diagram).* Make 23 blocks.

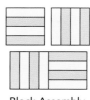

Block Assembly
Diagram

Block Diagram

Dark Strip Set Assembly

1. Referring to *Strip Set Chart* on page 76, make number of strip sets indicated, using assorted dark print strips.

2. Cut required number of segments from strip sets. Label segments A through I.

Strip Set Chart

Strip Set	A	B	C	D	E	F	G	H	I
Strips per Set	10	9	8	7	6	5	4	3	2
Number of Strip Sets	1	1	9	1	2	1	19	1	2
1½"-wide Segments	4	12	108	12	16	12	224	12	16

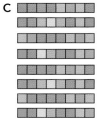

C

Corner Block
Assembly Diagram

Corner Block
Diagram

Setting Triangle Assembly

1. Lay out 1 each dark segments B through I and 1 dark print J square as shown in *Setting Unit Diagrams*. Join to complete 1 Setting Unit. Make 12 Setting Units.

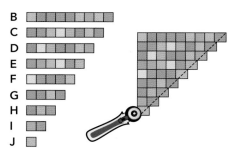

Setting Unit Diagrams

2. Trim long side of each Setting Unit to complete Setting Triangle, leaving ¼" seam allowance beyond points of squares as shown.

Corner Triangle Assembly

1. Join 1 each dark segments A, C, E, G, and I as shown in *Corner Unit Diagrams*.

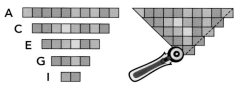

Corner Unit Diagrams

2. Trim short sides of Corner Unit, leaving ¼" seam allowance beyond points of squares as shown. Make 4 Corner Units.

Corner Block Assembly

1. Join 8 dark C segments as shown in *Corner Block Assembly Diagram*. Join segments to complete 1 Corner block (*Corner Block Diagram*). Make 4 Corner blocks.

Border Assembly

1. Join 2 (1½"-wide) light strip set segments and 2 dark G segments as shown in *Border Unit Diagrams*. Make 104 Border Units.

Quilt Top Assembly Diagram

G

Border Unit Diagrams

2. Join 32 Border Units as shown in *Quilt Top Assembly Diagram* to complete 1 side border. Make 2 side borders.

3. Join 20 Border Units to make top border. Repeat for bottom border.

Quilt Assembly

1. Lay out blocks, 60 C sashing segments, 38 J squares, Setting Units, and Corner Units as shown in *Quilt Top Assembly Diagram*. Join into diagonal rows; join rows to complete quilt center.

2. Press taupe print flange strips in half lengthwise, wrong sides facing.

3. Baste side flange strips to quilt center, aligning raw edges. Baste top and bottom flange strips to quilt.

4. Add side borders to quilt center.

5. Add Corner blocks to ends of top and bottom borders. Add borders to quilt.

Finishing

1. Divide backing into 2 (2½–yard) lengths. Cut 1 piece in half lengthwise to make 2 narrow panels. Join 1 narrow panel to each side of wider panel; press seam allowances toward narrow panels.

2. Layer backing, batting, and quilt top; baste. Quilt as desired. Quilt shown was quilted with a cable design in the blocks, straight lines through sashing and setting triangles, and bands of meandering in border *(Quilting Diagram)*.

3. Join 2¼"-wide taupe print strips into 1 continuous piece for straight-grain French-fold binding. Add binding to quilt.

Quilting Diagram

DESIGNER

Kim Cairns started sewing clothing as a 4-H member when she was nine years old. Now, as a sales representative for EE Schenck, she designs quilts showcasing their new lines of fabric. ❋

Shiloh

A Civil War era quilt in the Smithsonian Institution collection inspired both
the colors and the jagged edges in Julie Larsen's quilt. Her unique method for making Pineapple
blocks uses no templates, paper foundations, or special rulers.

PROJECT RATING: INTERMEDIATE

Size: 68" × 68"

Blocks: 25 (12") Pineapple blocks
3 (12½") setting blocks

MATERIALS

28 fat eighths★ assorted dark prints
  for block corners
20 fat quarters★★ assorted light
  prints for block backgrounds
2¼ yards black solid for block
  centers and outside corners
¾ yard dark print for binding
4¼ yards backing fabric
Twin-size quilt batting
★fat eighth = 9" × 20"
★★fat quarter = 18" × 20"

Cutting

Because the blocks have so many pieces
which are similar in size, you may want
to label them as you cut. Measurements
include ¼" seam allowances.

**From each dark print fat eighth, cut
  the following for block corners:**

• 4 (3½") E squares.
• 4 (3") D squares.

• 4 (2½") C squares.
• 4 (1½") B squares.

**From each light print fat quarter, cut
the following for regular blocks:**

• 11 (1½"-wide strips). From strips, cut:
  • 3 (1½" × 12½") K rectangles.
  • 5 (1½" × 10½") J rectangles.
  • 5 (1½" × 8½") I rectangles.
  • 5 (1½" × 6½") H rectangles.
  • 3 (1½" × 4½") G rectangles.
(You will have some extra pieces.)

**From remaining light print fabric
scraps, cut the following for setting blocks:**

• 6 (1½" × 13") Q rectangles.
• 12 (1½" × 11") P rectangles.
• 12 (1½" × 9") O rectangles.
• 12 (1½" × 7") N rectangles.
• 6 (1½" × 5") M rectangles.

From black solid, cut:

• 1 (5"-wide) strip. From strip, cut 3
  (5") L squares.
• 4 (4½"-wide) strips. From strips, cut
  25 (4½") A squares.
• 12 (4"-wide) strips. From strips, cut
  112 (4") F squares.

From dark print, cut:

• 10 (2¼"-wide) strips for binding.

Block Assembly

1. Referring to *Center Unit Diagrams*,
place 1 dark B square atop 1 black A
square, right sides facing. Join using
diagonal seams method—stitch diagonally from corner to corner, trim ¼"
beyond stitching, and press open to
reveal triangle. Repeat for remaining
3 corners to complete center unit.

Center Unit Diagrams

2. Join 1 G rectangle to top and bottom
of center unit (*Round 1 Diagrams* on
page 80). Join 1 H rectangle to each
side of unit. Using diagonal seams
method, join 1 C square to each corner to complete round 1.

3. Join 1 H rectangle to top and bottom
of round 1 unit (*Round 2 Diagrams*
on page 80). Join 1 I rectangle to
each side of unit. Using diagonal
seams method, join 1 D square to
each corner to complete round 2.

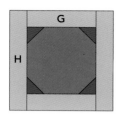
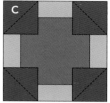
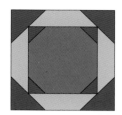

Round 1 Diagrams

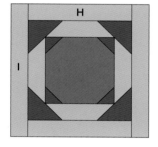
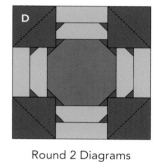
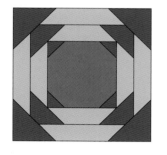

Round 2 Diagrams

Quilt Assembly

1. Referring to *Quilt Top Assembly Diagram*, lay out Pineapple blocks and setting squares as shown.

2. Join into diagonal rows; join rows to complete quilt top.

Finishing

1. Divide backing fabric into 2 (2⅛-yard) pieces. Cut 1 piece in half lengthwise to make 2 narrow panels. Sew 1 narrow panel to each side of wider panel; press seam allowances toward narrow panels.

4. Referring to *Pineapple Block Diagram*, continue in same manner to add rounds 3 and 4 to complete 1 Pineapple block. Make 25 Pineapple blocks.

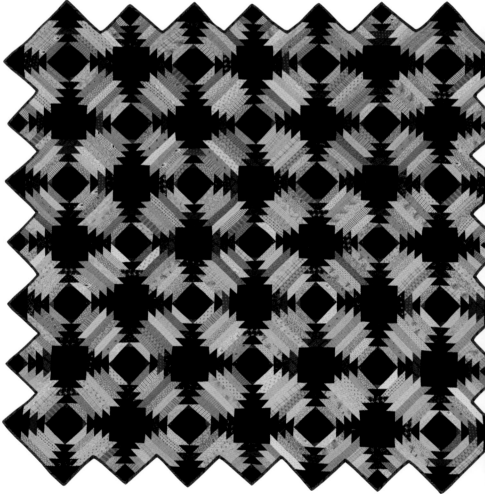

Pineapple Block Diagram

5. Repeat steps #1–#4 using pieces listed in *Setting Block Diagrams* to complete 1 setting block. Make 3 setting blocks.

6. Cut each setting block in half in both directions as shown in *Setting Block Diagrams* to make 12 setting squares.

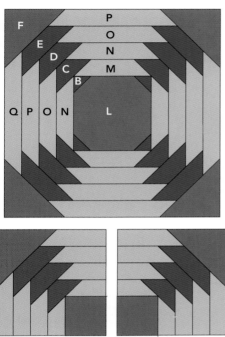

Setting Block Diagrams

Quilt Top Assembly Diagram

2. Layer backing, batting, and quilt top; baste. Quilt as desired. Quilt shown was hand quilted in the ditch along dark strips and down the center of light strips.

3. Join 2¼"-wide dark print binding strips into 1 continuous piece for straight-grain French-fold binding. Add binding to quilt.

TRIED & TRUE

This scrappy plaid set of 4 blocks was made by Shon McMain from Moda's "Linen Mate Plaid" and "Butternut and Blue" collections

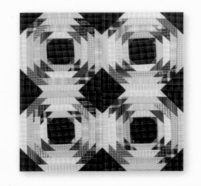

DESIGNER

Julie Larsen enjoys using innovative methods to create traditional quilts. She owns the award-winning quilt shop, Prairie Star Quilts in Elk Horn, Iowa. ✳

QUILT DESIGNED BY **Melanie Hurlston and Rosalie Quinlan.**
MADE BY **Melanie Hurlston.** MACHINE QUILTED BY **Around the Block Quilting.**

Seams of Opal

Choose an assortment of fun fat quarters to make these vibrant Log Cabin blocks. Use paper foundations to accurately piece the small blocks.

PROJECT RATING: EASY
Size: 74" × 74"
Blocks: 100 (5") Log Cabin blocks

MATERIALS

24 fat quarters★ assorted prints
3¼ yards white solid for sashing and border
¾ yard red print for binding
Paper for foundation piecing
4½ yards backing fabric
Full-size quilt batting
★fat quarter = 18" × 20"

Cutting

Measurements include ¼" seam allowances. Border strips are exact length needed. You may want to make them longer to allow for piecing variations. Pattern for Log Cabin block foundation is on page 84.

NOTE: For instructions on paper foundation piecing, see *Sew Easy: Log Cabin Foundation Piecing* on page 87.

From each of 15 assorted fat quarters, cut:

- 1 (2½"-wide) strip. From strip, cut 7 (2½") center squares.
- 1 (1½"-wide) strip. From strip, cut 6 (1½") sashing squares.
- 12 (1"-wide) strips.

From each remaining fat quarter, cut:

- 13 (1"-wide) strips.

From white solid, cut:

- 7 (5½"-wide) strips. From strips, cut 180 (5½" × 1½") sashing rectangles.
- 8 (8"-wide) strips. Piece strips to make 2 (8" × 74½") top and bottom borders and 2 (8" × 59½") side borders.

From red print, cut:

- 9 (2¼"-wide) strips for binding.

Block Assembly

1. Trace or photocopy 100 Log Cabin block foundations.

2. Starting with center square, foundation piece blocks in numerical order, using assorted prints *(Block Diagram)*. For detailed instructions, see *Sew Easy: Log Cabin Foundation Piecing* on page 87. Make 100 blocks.

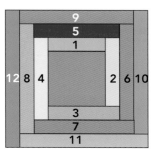

Block Diagram

Quilt Assembly

1. Lay out blocks, white sashing rectangles, and assorted sashing squares as shown in *Quilt Top Assembly Diagram* on page 85.

2. Join into rows; join rows to complete quilt center.

3. Add side borders to quilt center. Add top and bottom borders to quilt.

Finishing

1. Divide backing into 2 (2¼-yard) lengths. Cut 1 piece in half lengthwise to make 2 narrow panels. Join 1 narrow panel to each side of wider panel; press seam allowances toward narrow panels.

2. Layer backing, batting, and quilt top; baste. Quilt as desired. Quilt shown was quilted with an allover design *(Quilting Diagram on page 85)*.

3. Join 2¼"-wide red print strips into 1 continuous piece for straight-grain French-fold binding. Add binding to quilt.

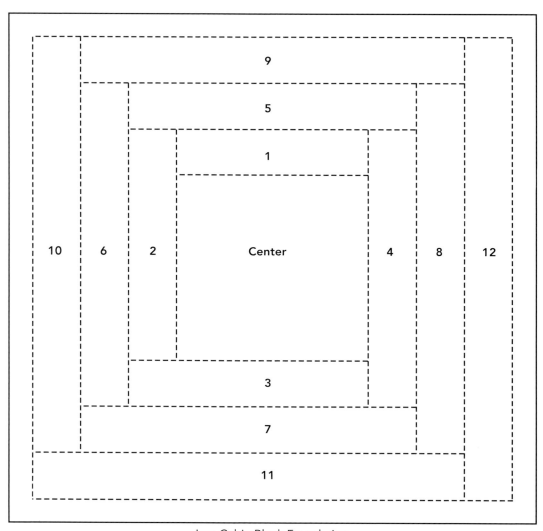

Log Cabin Block Foundation

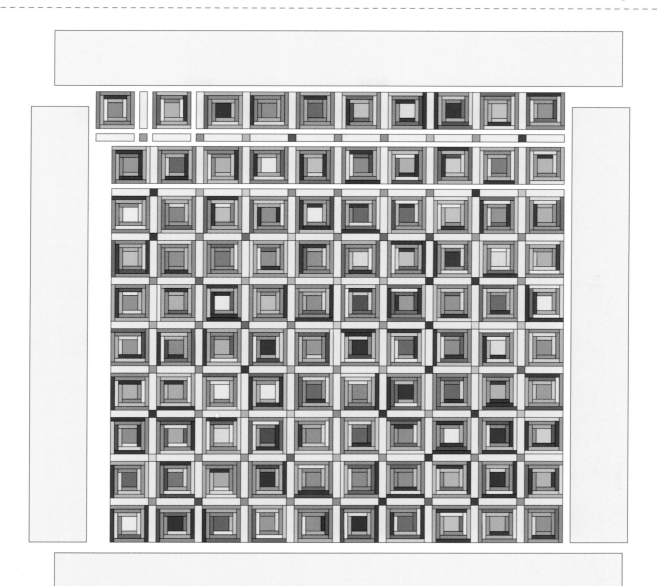

Quilt Top Assembly Diagram

Quilting Diagram

TRIED & TRUE

Our Log Cabin blocks feature coordinated fabrics from the In Full Bloom collection by Jill Kemp for Red Rooster Fabrics.

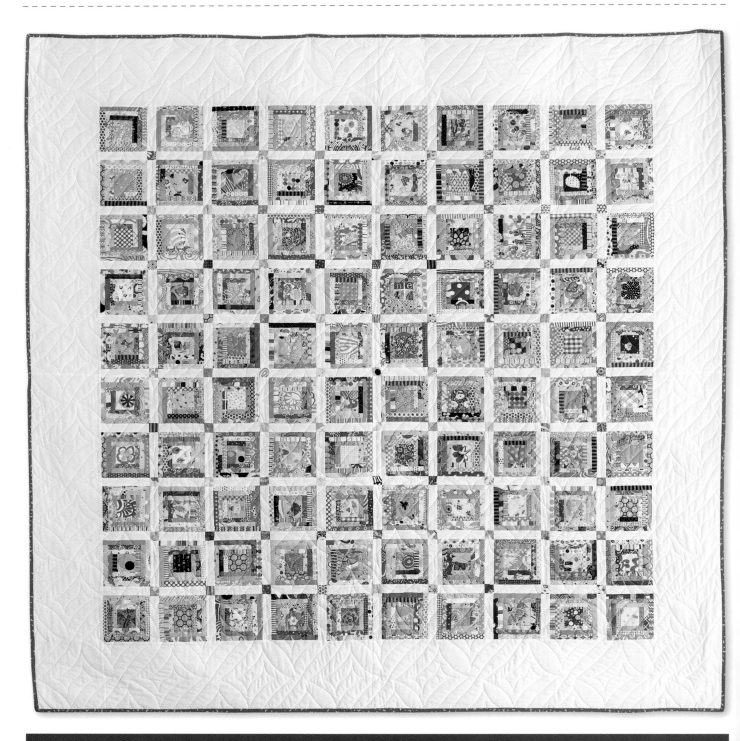

DESIGNER

Aussie sisters Melanie Hurlston and Rosalie Quinlan design together under the label Melly and Me. Their company produces easy-to-follow patterns for whimsical and contemporary toys, purses, and quilts. A love of fun fabrics, vibrant colors, and things that make them laugh is their common thread. ✳

Sew Easy™
Log Cabin Foundation Piecing

Use this method to accurately make small Log Cabin blocks such as those in *Seams of Opal* on page 82.

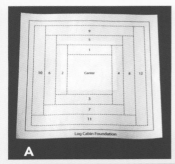

A

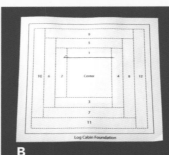

B

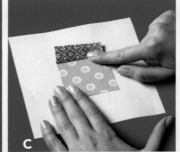

C

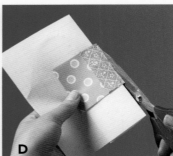

D

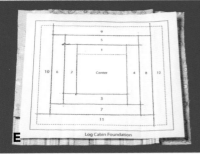

E

F

G

1. Using ruler and pencil, trace all lines and the outer edge of the foundation pattern onto tracing paper. Number the pieces to indicate the stitching order.

Sew Smart™
Save time by making photocopies on special foundation papers. Check photocopied patterns to be sure they are correct size. (Some copiers may distort copy size.) —Marianne

2. Using fabric pieces that are larger than the numbered areas, place fabrics for center and #1 right sides facing, with center piece on top. Position paper pattern atop fabrics with printed side of paper facing you (*Photo A*). Make sure the fabric for center is under that area and that edges of fabrics extend at least ⅛" beyond stitching line between section #1 and center.

3. Using a short machine stitch so papers will tear off easily later, stitch on line between the two sections, extending stitching into seam allowances at ends of seams (*Photo B*). Trim #1 strip at end of stitching.

4. Open out pieces and press or finger press the seam (*Photo C*).
The right sides of the fabric pieces will be facing out on the back side of the paper pattern.

5. Flip the work over and fold back paper pattern on stitched line. Trim seam allowance to ⅛", being careful not to cut paper pattern (*Photo D*).

6. Continue to add pieces in numerical order and trim strips as necessary until pattern is covered. Use rotary cutter and ruler to trim excess paper and fabric along outer pattern lines (*Photos E, F, and G*).

7. Carefully tear off foundation paper after blocks are joined.

Stepping Out in Color

Flavin Glover designed this unique Log Cabin quilt with exploding bursts of color that appear to float on a background of black prints.

PROJECT RATING: CHALLENGING
Size: 78" × 78"
Blocks: 100 (9" × 4½") Courthouse Steps blocks

MATERIALS

40 fat eighths★ assorted prints in red, orange, yellow, green, purple, and blue
26 fat quarters★★ assorted black prints
¾ yard pink print for border
½ yard yellow print for border
¾ yard multi-color stripe for border
1 yard black print for border
¾ yard purple print for binding
7⅛ yards backing fabric
Full-size quilt batting
★fat eighth = 9" × 20"
★★fat quarter = 18" × 20"

Cutting

Measurements include ¼" seam allowances. Because there are so many pieces which are similar in size, you may want to label them as you cut.

From fat eighths, cut:
• (1¼"-wide) strips. From strips, cut logs as listed in *Cutting Chart for Blocks.*

Sew **Smart**™

To avoid stretching or distortion of narrow logs, cut strips on the lengthwise grain of the fabric (parallel to the selvages). —Flavin

From fat quarters, cut:
• (1¼"-wide) strips. From strips, cut logs as listed in *Cutting Chart for Blocks.*

Sew **Smart**™

Cutting logs to specified lengths prior to construction can aid in block accuracy and enable you to machine piece multi-fabric blocks more quickly. —Flavin

From pink print, cut:
• 9 (2½"-wide) strips. Piece strips to make 4 (2½" × 84") strips for borders.

From yellow print, cut:
• 9 (1½"-wide) strips. Piece strips to make 4 (1½" × 84") strips for borders.

CUTTING CHART FOR BLOCKS

Cut All Strips 1¼" wide

		Piece #	Length	Color	Black
	Center	C	2"	320	480
	Accent	8	5"	100	—
Set A		1	6½"	64	36
Set A		3	3½"	64	36
Set A		5	8"	64	36
Set A		7	5"	64	36
Set B		2	6½"	—	100
Set B		4	3½"	—	100
Set B		6	8"	—	100

From multi-color stripe, cut:
- 9 (2"-wide) strips. Piece strips to make 4 (2" × 84") strips for borders.

From black print, cut:
- 9 (3"-wide) strips. Piece strips to make 4 (3" × 84") strips for borders.

From purple print, cut:
- 9 (2¼"-wide) strips for binding.

Block Assembly

1. Lay out 3 assorted black C pieces and 5 assorted orange C pieces as shown in *Center Unit Assembly Diagrams.* Join pieces to make 1 orange Center Unit.

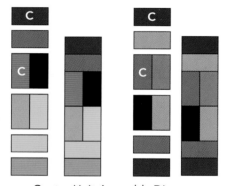

Center Unit Assembly Diagrams

2. Select 1 Set A of orange logs (#1, #3, #5, #7) and 1 Set B of black logs (#2, #4, #6) and 1 purple accent log (#8). Referring to *Block Diagrams*, add logs to orange Center Unit in numerical order to complete 1 orange block.

> ## Sew **Smart**™
> **Refer to photo on page 92 and *Quilt Top Assembly Diagram* on page 91 for color placement in rectangular Courthouse Steps blocks. You may download a *Block Placement Diagram* at Fonsand-Porter.com/socbpd.**

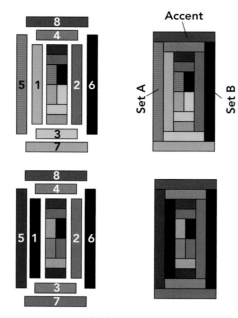

Block Diagrams

3. Repeat steps #1 and #2 to make 4 orange blocks, selecting accent log color (#8) referring to photo on page 92, *Quilt Top Assembly Diagram* on page 91, or your *Block Placement Diagram.*

4. In the same manner make 16 sets of 4 blocks, referring to *Quilt Top Assembly Diagram* or your Block Placement Diagram for color selection.

5. Lay out 8 assorted black C pieces as shown in *Center Unit Assembly Diagrams.* Join pieces to make 1 black Center Unit.

6. Select 1 Set A of black logs (#1, #3, #5, #7), 1 Set B of black logs (#2, #4, #6), and 1 purple accent log (#8). Referring to *Block Diagrams*, add logs to black block center in numerical order to complete 1 black block.

7. Repeat steps #5 and #6 to make 36 black blocks, selecting accent log color (#8) referring to *Quilt Top Assembly Diagram* on page 91 or your *Block Placement Diagram.*

8. Join 2 black blocks to make a square as shown in *Setting Triangle Diagrams.* Cut square in half diagonally to make 2 half-square setting triangles. Repeat to make 20 half-square setting triangles.

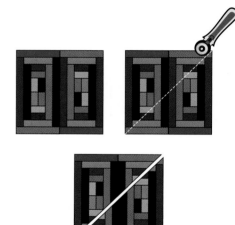

Setting Triangle Diagrams

Quilt Assembly

1. Lay out blocks and setting triangles as shown in *Quilt Top Assembly Diagram.*

2. Join into diagonal rows, beginning at upper left and working to lower right.

3. Join rows to complete quilt center.

4. Join 1 pink print, 1 yellow print, 1 stripe, and 1 black print border strips as shown in *Quilt Top Assembly Diagram.* Repeat to make 4 border strip sets.

5. Add border strip sets to quilt, mitering corners. For detailed instructions, see *Sew Easy: Mitered Borders* on page 93.

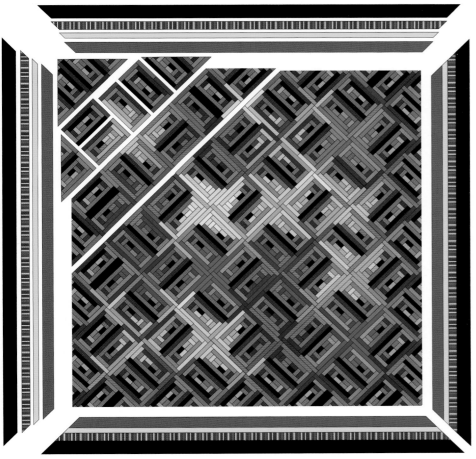

Quilt Top Assembly Diagram

Quilting Diagram

Finishing

1. Divide backing fabric into 3 (2⅜-yard) lengths. Join panels lengthwise.

2. Layer backing, batting, and quilt top; baste. Quilt as desired. Quilt shown was quilted in the ditch in the borders, setting triangles, and black Log Cabin blocks and with a whirligig design in the color Log Cabin blocks *(Quilting Diagram)*.

3. Join 2¼"-wide purple print strips into 1 continuous piece for straight-grain French-fold binding. Add binding to quilt.

TRIED & TRUE

Flavin made a more masculine version of this quilt using varied shades of denim.

DESIGNER

Flavin Glover's trademark quilts are innovative Log Cabin and geometric patchwork composed of many fabrics in vibrant colors. Her *Row Houses* was included in *100 Best American Quilts of the 20th Century.* Flavin's Log Cabin landscape and architectural quilts are also featured in her book, *A New Look at Log Cabin Quilts,* from C&T Publishing. ✳

Mitered Borders

The subtle seam of a mitered corner creates the illusion of a continuous line around the quilt. Mitered corners are ideal for striped fabric borders or multiple plain borders.

1. Referring to *Measuring Diagram*, measure your quilt length through the middle of the quilt rather than along the edges. In the same manner, measure quilt width. Add to your measurements twice the planned width of the border plus 2". Trim borders to these measurements.

Measuring Diagram

2. On wrong side of quilt top, mark ¼" seam allowances at each corner.

3. Fold quilt top in half and place a pin at the center of the quilt side. Fold border in half and mark center with pin.

4. With right sides facing and raw edges aligned, match center pins on the border and the quilt. Working from the center out, pin the border to the quilt, right sides facing. The border will extend beyond the quilt edges. Do not trim the border.

5. Sew the border to the quilt. Start and stop stitching ¼" from the corner of the quilt top, backstitching at each end. Press the seam allowance toward the border. Add the remaining borders in the same manner.

6. With right sides facing, fold the quilt diagonally as shown in *Mitering Diagram 1*, aligning the raw edges of the adjacent borders. Pin securely.

7. Align a ruler along the diagonal fold, as shown in *Mitering Diagram 2*. Holding the ruler firmly, mark a line from the end of the border seam to the raw edge.

8. Start machine-stitching at the beginning of the marked line, backstitch, and then stitch on the line out to the raw edge.

9. Unfold the quilt to be sure that the corner lies flat (*Mitered Borders Diagram*). Correct the stitching if necessary. Trim the seam allowance to ¼".

10. Miter the remaining corners. Press the corner seams open.

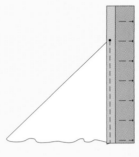

Mitering Diagram 1

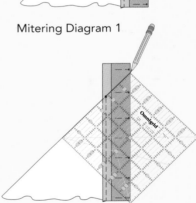

Mitering Diagram 2

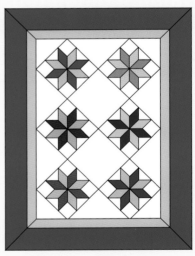

Mitered Borders Diagram

Magic Triangles

Easy strip piecing makes this striking quilt a great weekend project. Use a collection of graphic black-and-white prints to create contrast and interest.

PROJECT RATING: INTERMEDIATE
Size: 73¼" × 73¼"
Blocks: 41 (9") blocks

MATERIALS

- 1⅛ yards black-and-white stripe for blocks and inner border
- 2 yards black solid for blocks, outer border, and binding
- ⅝ yard each of 10 assorted light, medium, and dark prints in black, gray, and white
- Fons & Porter Half & Quarter Ruler or template plastic
- 4½ yards backing fabric
- Full-size quilt batting

Cutting

Measurements include ¼" seam allowances. Border strips are exact length needed. You may want to make them longer to allow for piecing variations. Instructions are written for using the Fons & Porter Half & Quarter Ruler. If not using this ruler, cut a 7¼" square from template plastic. Cut square in half diagonally for template. Mark tip ⅛" from point and cut it off.

From black-and-white stripe, cut:
- 8 (2"-wide) strips. Piece strips to make 4 (2" × 76") inner borders.

From black solid, cut:
- 8 (3¾"-wide) strips. Piece strips to make 4 (3¾" × 76") outer borders.
- 8 (2¼"-wide) strips for binding.

From assorted fabrics including black-and-white stripe and black solid, cut a total of:
NOTE: Cut all strips in sets of 2 matching strips.
- 8 (2⅛"-wide) strips.
- 38 (2"-wide) strips. **NOTE:** At least 12 of these 2"-wide strips should be from the darkest fabrics and 6 from medium and light fabrics for setting triangles.
- 12 (1¾"-wide) strips.
- 16 (1⅝"-wide) strips.
- 32 (1½"-wide) strips.
- 12 (1¼"-wide) strips.
- 8 (1⅛"-wide) strips.
- 8 (1"-wide) strips.

Setting Triangle Assembly

1. Join 2 dark 2"-wide strips and 1 light 2"-wide strip as shown in *Strip Set #1 Diagram*. Press all seams in same direction. Make 6 Strip Set #1 in 3 sets of 2 identical strip sets.

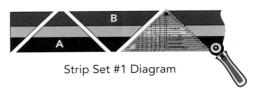

Strip Set #1 Diagram

2. Using the Fons & Porter Half & Quarter Ruler or template, cut 3 A triangles and 3 B triangles from each strip set as shown.
NOTE: A and B triangles are the same size. A triangles are cut from the bottom of the strip set and B triangles are cut from the top of the strip set.

3. Join 2 matching A triangles as shown in *Side Setting Triangle Diagrams* on page 96. Make 8 Side Setting Triangles. In the same manner, make 8 Side Setting Triangles using matching pairs of B triangles. Remaining triangles are Corner Setting Triangles.

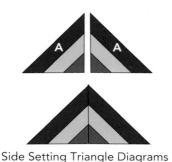

Side Setting Triangle Diagrams

Block Assembly

1. Referring to *Strip Set Diagrams #1–#7*, use assorted print, stripe, and solid strips to make 4 each of strip sets #1–#7 in sets of 2 identical strip sets.

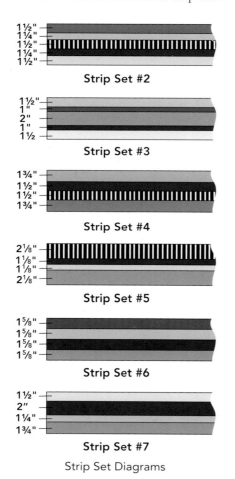

1½"
1¼"
1½"
1¼"
1½"

Strip Set #2

1½"
1"
2"
1"
1½"

Strip Set #3

1¾"
1½"
1½"
1¾"

Strip Set #4

2⅛"
1⅛"
1⅛"
2⅛"

Strip Set #5

1⅝"
1⅝"
1⅝"
1⅝"

Strip Set #6

1½"
2"
1¼"
1¾"

Strip Set #7

Strip Set Diagrams

2. Using the Fons & Porter Half & Quarter Ruler or template, cut 3 A triangles and 3 B triangles from each strip set. Keep triangles in matching pairs.

NOTE: Triangle pairs must be joined with triangle pairs of the same strip set number so the seams will match. For blocks #1–#6, A triangles can be used with B triangles. For block #7, 4 A triangles or 4 B triangles must be used.

3. Join pairs of triangles to make 41 blocks *(Block Diagrams)*. You will have 2 pairs of triangles left over.

Quilt Assembly

1. Lay out blocks and setting triangles as shown in *Quilt Top Assembly Diagram*. Join into diagonal rows; join rows to complete quilt center.

2. Join 1 inner border and 1 outer border as shown in *Quilt Top Assembly Diagram*. Make 4 borders.

3. Add borders to quilt center, mitering corners. For detailed instructions, see *Sew Easy: Mitered Borders* on page 93.

Block #1

Block #2

Block #3

Block #4

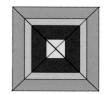

Block #5

Block #6

Block #7

Block Diagrams

Quilt Top Assembly Diagram

Finishing

1. Divide backing into 2 (2¼-yard) lengths. Cut 1 piece in half lengthwise to make 2 narrow panels. Join 1 narrow panel to each side of wider panel; press seam allowances toward narrow panels.

2. Layer backing, batting, and quilt top; baste. Quilt as desired. Quilt shown was quilted in the ditch and with diagonal lines in the outer border *(Quilting Diagram)*.

3. Join 2¼"-wide black solid strips into 1 continuous piece for straight-grain French-fold binding. Add binding to quilt.

Quilting Diagram

DESIGNER

Lynda Faires grew up sewing, and says she loves fabric. She makes wearable art, art quilts, bed quilts, and mixed media collages. Lynda teaches and exhibits nationally and internationally. ✳

TRIED & TRUE

Pink and green prints, stripes, plaids, and florals lend a soft look to this geometric design. We used fabrics from the Blossoms (Simply Simple Quilts) line by Ro Gregg for Northcott.

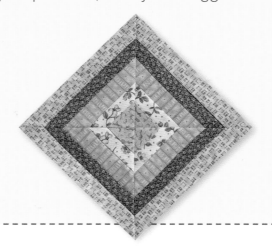

Flannel Jacks

Designer Shon McMain tamed the stretchy nature of flannel fabrics by piecing on muslin foundation squares. She says, "I knew I wouldn't be able to keep the lines within the plaids straight on traditional Log Cabin blocks so I decided to make crazy ones. I used both purchased flannels and fabric rescued from old flannel shirts."

PROJECT RATING: INTERMEDIATE
Size: 70¼" × 84½"
Blocks: 20 (13") Crazy Cabin blocks

MATERIALS

36 fat quarters★ assorted plaid flannels

4 yards 45"-wide muslin for block and border foundation

1⅞ yards black solid flannel for center triangles, sashing, inner border, and binding

5 yards backing fabric

Full-size quilt batting

★fat quarter = 18" × 20"

Cutting

Measurements include ¼" seam allowances. Border strips are exact length needed. You may want to make them longer to allow for piecing variations.

From each plaid flannel fat quarter, cut:

• 1 or 2 (1½"-, 2"-, 2½"-, and 3"-wide) strips.

From muslin, cut:

• 2 (13½"-wide) **lengthwise** strips. From strips, cut 20 (13½") squares and 4 (6½") squares for block foundations.

• 2 (6½") **lengthwise** strips. From strips, cut 2 (6½" × 73") side border foundations and 2 (6½" × 58¾") top and bottom border foundations.

From black solid flannel, cut:

• 1 (6"-wide) strip. From strip, cut 5 (6" × 7") rectangles. Cut rectangles into triangles following the instructions in Step #1 of *Sew Easy: Piecing Crazy Log Cabin Blocks* on page 101.

• 9 (2½"-wide) strips for binding.

> ## Sew **Smart**™
> When making flannel quilts, I like to cut binding strips 2½" wide. —Liz

• 21 (1¾"-wide) strips. Piece 13 strips to make 6 (1¾" × 55¼") horizontal sashing strips and 2 (1¾" × 73"), vertical sashing strips. From remaining 8 strips, cut 15 (1¾" × 13½") sashing strips.

From remainder of black flannel, cut:

• 2 (2¾" × 2¼") rectangles. Cut rectangles in half diagonally to make corner triangle centers.

Block Assembly

Note: To make Crazy Cabin blocks, follow the instructions in *Sew Easy: Piecing Crazy Log Cabin Blocks* on page 101.

1. Make 20 Crazy Cabin blocks.

2. Make 4 Crazy Cabin border corner blocks, using small black triangles and 6½" muslin foundation squares.

Border Assembly

1. Place 1 strip of plaid right side up and crosswise near the center of 1 muslin border strip.

2. With right sides facing and long raw edges aligned, pin a second flannel strip atop first strip. Stitch through all layers, with a ¼" seam.

3. Open out the top (second) strip; press. Trim ends of strips even with long edges of muslin foundation.

4. Continue adding strips, working from both sides of beginning strip, until muslin foundation fabric is covered.

5. Trim excess strips even with edges of muslin foundation.

6. Repeat to make 4 borders.

Quilt Assembly

1. Referring to *Quilt Top Assembly Diagram*, lay out Crazy Cabin blocks and sashing strips as shown. Join into rows; join rows to complete quilt center.

2. Add side borders to quilt center.

3. Add 1 corner block to each end of the top and bottom borders. Add borders to quilt.

Quilting and Finishing

1. Divide backing fabric into 2 (2½-yard) lengths. Cut 1 piece in half lengthwise. Sew 1 narrow panel to each side of wider panel. Press seam allowances toward narrow panels.

2. Layer backing, batting, and quilt top; baste. Quilt as desired. Quilt shown was machine quilted ¼" inside the black sashing seams and with meandering in the blocks and borders.

3. Join 2½"-wide black strips into 1 continuous piece for straight-grain French-fold binding. Add binding to quilt.

Quilt Top Assembly Diagram

DESIGNER

Whether she's choosing fabrics, creating original designs, piecing, or quilting, designer Shon McMain loves every aspect of making quilts. Most of her quilts are made from batiks, her favorite fabrics. Shon lives in Des Moines, Iowa, and is a frequent contributor to *Love of Quilting*.

Sew Easy™

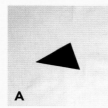 **A** 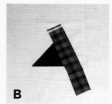 **B**  **C**  **D**

Piecing Crazy Log Cabin Blocks

This fun patchwork method results in Log Cabin blocks that are each unique. Begin with any straight-sided shape for the center and then work the patchwork around that shape. Shon McMain used triangles for the centers of all of her blocks. Follow the easy steps below to learn this method.

Materials

1 (13½") muslin square for foundation
1 (6" × 7") rectangle black fabric
Assorted fabric strips ranging from
    1½"–3" wide

Instructions

1. To create a triangular center shape, cut black rectangle in half diagonally. Cut each half in 2 pieces, cutting from right angle corner to a spot at least 2½" away from 1 of the other corners, making each resulting triangle slightly different (*Triangle Cutting Diagrams*).

Triangle Cutting Diagrams

2. Center 1 black triangle right side up on 13½" square of muslin (*Photo A*). Save extra triangles to make additional blocks.

3. Pin a plaid strip atop black triangle, right sides facing, aligning raw edge of strip with 1 side of triangle and allowing

about 3" of strip to extend beyond corners of triangle. Stitch through all layers along length of triangle side, with ¼" seam (*Photo B*).

4. Open out strip; press seam allowances toward strip. In a similar manner, add a second strip to an adjacent side of black triangle, extending stitching across end of first strip (*Photo C*). Trim end of first strip even with edge of second strip.

5. Add a third strip to the remaining side of the triangle, extending stitching across ends of first two strips. This completes one round of patchwork (*Photo D*).

6. Repeat steps #2–#5, continuing in the same direction around the center. Add various colors and widths of strips in each round. When you can no longer make complete rounds, add strips to fill corner areas. Muslin foundation square should be completely covered with strips (*Photo E*).

> ## Sew Smart™
> Some of the plaid strips can be sewn on at a slight angle to give the Crazy Logs an even "crazier" look. —Liz

7. Using a rotary cutter and ruler, trim strips even with sides of muslin foundation square (*Photo F*).

> ## Sew Smart™
> Use a regular ruler or a large square ruler to trim the blocks. —Marianne

8. Completed block, including seam allowances should measure 13½" square. Make desired number of blocks, varying strip arrangement (*Photo G*).

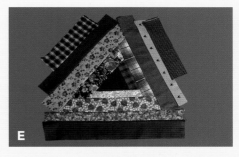

E

F

G

Wheels for Mary

Mary Mashuta combined Hungarian blue print fabrics with stripes from her personal feed sack collection to make her Wagon Wheel blocks. She embellished her quilt with buttons, rickrack, and yo-yos. See *Sew Easy: Making Yo-Yos* on page 107 to learn this method for making the block centers.

PROJECT RATING: CHALLENGING
Size: 53½" × 54⅛"
Blocks: 22 (8½" × 9¾") Wagon Wheel blocks

MATERIALS

8 fat quarters★ assorted stripes for blocks
8 fat quarters★ assorted dark blue prints for blocks
5 fat quarters★ assorted red checks for block centers
⅝ yard navy blue print for outer border
1½ yards light blue diagonal plaid for inner border
6" square dark blue plaid for inner border corners
½ yard red check for binding
3½ yards backing fabric
Fons & Porter's Wagon Wheel Template set or template material
6½ yards red jumbo rickrack
24 (¾"–1"-diameter) assorted red buttons
Twin-size quilt batting
★fat quarter = 18" × 20"

Cutting

If you are not using the Fons & Porter's Wagon Wheel Template Set, make templates from the patterns on page 105. Punch hole in B template at point indicated by dot on pattern piece. Measurements include ¼" seam allowances.

From each stripe fat quarter, cut:

• 24 A.

From each dark blue print fat quarter, cut:

• 24 B.

From each red check fat quarter, cut:

• 4 Centers. (You will have a few extra.)

• 9 Yo-Yos. If you prefer to appliqué centers instead of using Yo-Yos, cut 9 Centers from each fat quarter. (You will have a few extra pieces.)

From navy blue print, cut:

• 5 (3¾"-wide) strips for outer border.

From light blue plaid, cut:

• 1 (3¾"-wide) strip. From strip, cut 4 (3¾") D squares.

• 4 (2¾"-wide) **lengthwise** strips for inner border.

From dark blue plaid, cut:

• 4 (2¾") C squares.

From red check, cut:

• 2¼"-wide bias strips. Join to make about 225" of bias for binding.

Wagon Wheel Assembly

1. Referring to *Block Assembly Diagrams*, choose 6 dark blue B pieces and 6 stripe A pieces; mark dot on each B piece. Join 3 A pieces and 3 B pieces to make a block half. Make 2 halves; join to complete 1 wheel.

2. Referring to *Sew Easy: Making Yo-Yos* on page 107, make 22 Yo-Yos for block centers. (If you prefer, cut Centers to appliqué on blocks.) Appliqué 1 Yo-Yo or 1 Center on

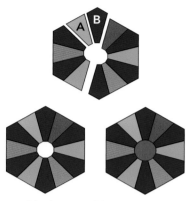

Block Assembly Diagrams

wheel to complete 1 Wagon Wheel block. Make 22 blocks.

3. In the same manner, make 10 X half blocks and 6 Y half blocks *(Half Block Diagrams)*.

X Half Block   **Y Half Block**

Half Block Diagrams

Quilt Top Assembly

1. Lay out blocks and half blocks as shown in *Quilt Top Assembly Diagram*. Join into horizontal rows, stitching from dot to dot and backstitching at dots; leave seam allowance free beyond dots. In the same manner, join rows to complete quilt center.

2. Trim edges of quilt top to straighten as shown in *Quilt Top Assembly Diagram*.

Quilt Top Assembly Diagram

3. Measure length of quilt center. Cut 2 side inner borders this measurement. Measure width of quilt center. Cut 2 top and bottom borders this measurement. Add side inner borders to quilt center. Join 1 dark blue plaid C square to each end of top and bottom borders. Add borders to quilt.

4. Join navy print strips into 1 continuous strip. Repeat step #3 to add outer borders to quilt, using D squares for corners.

Finishing

1. Divide backing into 2 (1¾-yard) pieces. Cut one piece in half lengthwise to make two narrow panels. Join one narrow panel to wider panel; press seam allowances toward narrow panel. Remaining panel is extra and can be used to make a hanging sleeve.

2. Layer backing, batting, and quilt top; baste. Quilt as desired. Quilt shown was outline quilted ¼" from seams and with a scallop in outer border.

3. Baste rickrack to quilt top, placing center of rickrack ¼" from edge of quilt.

4. Add binding to quilt, stitching through all layers.

5. Referring to photo on page 106, sew buttons on outer border.

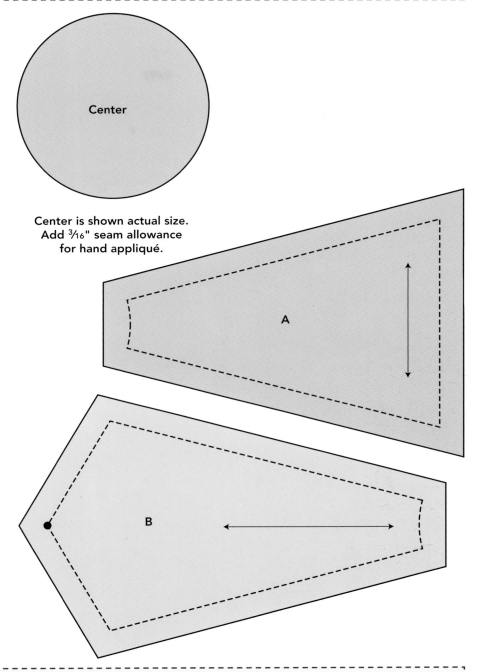

Center is shown actual size.
Add ³⁄₁₆" seam allowance
for hand appliqué.

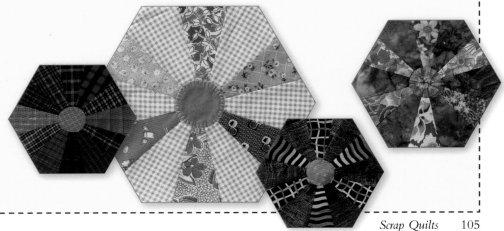

TRIED & TRUE

Mary made several blocks in alternate color combinations. Experiment with different types of fabrics to get a look that pleases you.

Sew *Easy*™

Making Yo-Yos

Mary placed yo-yos at the centers of her Wagon Wheel blocks, adding an element of fun and dimension to the quilt.

1. Cut a 5" circle using pattern at right.
2. Turn under raw edge of circle ¼" to wrong side and take small running stitches around edge through both layers (*Photo A*). Use quilting thread or other strong thread that will not break when gathered.
3. Pull thread to gather circle with right side of fabric out (*Photo B*). Make a knot to hold circle closed. Gathered side is front of yo-yo.

Sew **Smart**™
Do not make running stitches too small. Longer stitches make the circle easier to gather, and the "hole" smaller
—Marianne

Yo-Yo Circle

A

B

Thousand Pyramids

Pull batiks from your stash to make this dynamic quilt.

PROJECT RATING: INTERMEDIATE
Size: 82½" × 105"

MATERIALS

74 fat quarters★ assorted batiks in teal, blue, green, purple, pink, red, and brown
1 yard green batik for binding
Fons & Porter's 60° Pyramids Ruler or template plastic
7½ yards backing fabric
Queen-size quilt batting
★fat quarter = 18" × 20"

Cutting

Refer to *Sew Easy: Cutting 60° Diamonds and Pyramids* on page 113 for instructions to cut triangles. If you are not using Fons & Porter's Pyramids Ruler, make a template from the pattern on page 110. Measurements include ¼" seam allowances.

From each fat quarter, cut:
• 5 (3"-wide) strips. From strips, cut 36 triangles.

From green batik, cut:
• 2¼"-wide bias strips. Join to make about 460" of bias for binding.

Diamond Assembly

1. Choose 6 matching triangles and 3 similar color matching triangles as shown in *Large Triangle Assembly Diagram*. Join to make 1 large triangle *(Large Triangle Diagram)*. Make 294 large triangles.

Large Triangle Assembly Diagram

Large Triangle Diagram

2. Join 2 similar color large triangles to make 1 diamond *(Diamond Diagrams)*. Make 136 diamonds.

Diamond Diagrams

Quilt Assembly

1. Lay out diamonds and remaining large triangles as shown in *Quilt Top Assembly Diagram*.

2. Join into diagonal rows; join rows to complete quilt top.

Finishing

1. Divide backing fabric into 3 (2½-yard) lengths. Join panels length-wise. Seams will run horizontally.

2. Layer backing, batting, and quilt top; baste. Quilt as desired. Quilt shown was quilted with an allover freehand design *(Quilting Diagram)*.

3. Add binding to quilt.

Quilting Diagram

TRIED & TRUE

This traditional pattern looks great when made from 1930s reproduction prints.

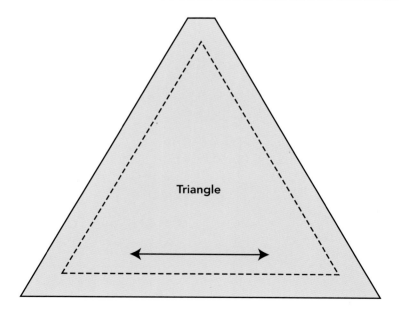

Triangle

Quilt Top Assembly Diagram

DESIGNER

Whether she's choosing fabrics, creating original designs, piecing, or quilting, designer Shon McMain loves every aspect of making quilts. Most of her quilts are made from batiks, her favorite fabrics. Shon lives in Des Moines, Iowa, and is a frequent contributor to *Love of Quilting*.

Sew *Easy*™

Cutting 60° Diamonds and Pyramids

Use the Fons & Porter 60° Diamonds Ruler and 60° Pyramids Ruler
to make easy work of cutting pieces.

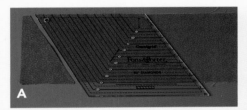

Diamonds

1. To cut diamonds, cut strip desired width (for *Katie's String Star* on page 152, cut strips 5¾" wide).

2. Referring to strip width numbers along lower section of Fons & Porter 60° Diamonds ruler, find the line on the ruler that corresponds to the width of strip you cut.

3. Beginning at left end of fabric strip, place ruler so bottom line for desired size diamond is aligned with bottom edge of strip, and cut along left side of ruler (*Photo A*).

Sew **Smart**™
To cut the maximum number of pieces from a fabric strip, open out the strip so you will be cutting through a single layer. To cut many pieces, layer several strips and cut them at the same time. —Liz

4. Move ruler to the right; align desired line of ruler with slanted edge and bottom edge of strip. Cut along right slanted edge of ruler to cut diamond (*Photo B*).

5. Repeat Step #4 to cut required number of diamonds.

Pyramids

1. To cut pyramids (triangles), cut strip desired width (for *Thousand Pyramids*, cut strips 3" wide; for *Katie's String Star* on page 152, cut strips 5¾" wide).

2. Referring to strip width numbers along lower section of Fons & Porter 60° Pyramids ruler, find the line on the ruler that corresponds to the width of strip you cut.

3. Beginning at left end of fabric strip, place ruler atop strip so line on ruler is along bottom edge of fabric strip. Trim along left slanted edge of ruler (*Photo C*).

Sew **Smart**™
If you cut left handed, work from the right end of the fabric strip and begin by cutting along the right edge of the ruler. —Marianne

4. Cut along right slanted edge of ruler to cut one pyramid triangle.

5. To cut second pyramid triangle, rotate ruler so solid line is on top edge of strip and angled side of ruler is aligned with slanted edge of strip. Cut along slanted edge of ruler (*Photo D*).

6. Continue in this manner to cut required number of Pyramids (*Photo E*).

Scrappy Diamonds

Bold, high-contrast fabrics give lots of character to this beautiful throw-size quilt you can piece in a weekend.

PROJECT RATING: EASY

Size: 57" × 69"

Blocks: 16 (10" × 13") Diamond blocks

MATERIALS

NOTE: Fabrics shown are from the Chocolate Lollipop collection by Free Spirit.

6 fat quarters★ assorted light prints for blocks

6 fat quarters★ assorted dark prints for blocks

⅜ yard medium brown print for inner border

1½ yards turquoise print for outer border

½ yard dark brown print for binding

3½ yards backing fabric

Twin-size quilt batting

★fat quarter = 18" × 20"

Cutting

Measurements include ¼" seam allowances. Border strips are exact length needed. You may want to make them longer to allow for piecing variations.

From each fat quarter, cut:

• 2 (7½"-wide) strips. From strips, cut 6 (7½" × 6") rectangles.

From medium brown print, cut:

• 5 (1½"-wide) strips. Piece strips to make 2 (1½" × 52½") side inner borders and 2 (1½" × 42½") top and bottom inner borders.

From turquoise print, cut:

• 6 (8"-wide) strips. Piece strips to make 2 (8" × 57½") top and bottom outer borders and 2 (8" × 54½") side outer borders.

From dark brown print, cut:

• 7 (2¼"-wide) strips for binding.

Block Assembly

1. Stack 4 assorted light print rectangles and 4 assorted dark print rectangles right sides up, with pieces aligned, alternating light prints and dark prints. Make 8 stacks.

2. Referring to *Rectangle Cutting Diagrams*, cut 4 stacks in half diagonally from lower right to upper left and cut 4 stacks in half diagonally from lower left to upper right as shown.

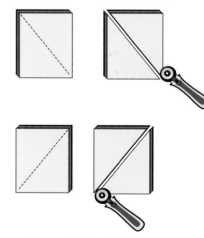

Rectangle Cutting Diagrams

3. Remove top triangle from 1 stack and place it on the bottom of the stack.

4. Join the 2 top triangles (one should be dark and the other one light) to make 1 pieced rectangle as shown

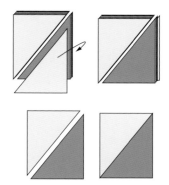

Pieced Rectangle Diagrams

in *Pieced Rectangle Diagrams*. Trim rectangle to 5½" × 7". Repeat with remaining triangles in stack to make 8 pieced rectangles.

5. In the same manner, make 8 pieced rectangles from each of the remaining 7 stacks.

6. Lay out 4 pieced rectangles as shown in *Block Assembly Diagram*. Join rectangles to complete 1 Diamond block *(Block Diagram)*. Make 16 Diamond blocks.

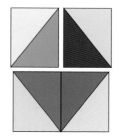

Block Assembly Diagram

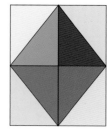

Block Diagram

Quilt Assembly

1. Lay out blocks as shown in *Quilt Top Assembly Diagram*.

2. Join into rows; join rows to complete quilt center.

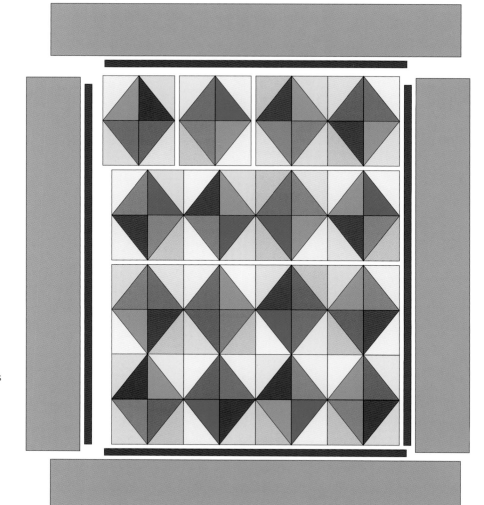

Quilt Top Assembly Diagram

> ## Sew **Smart**™
>
> **Press seams open when joining rectangles to eliminate bulk. —Liz**

3. Add medium brown print side inner borders to quilt center. Add medium brown print top and bottom inner borders to quilt. Repeat for turquoise print outer borders.

Finishing

1. Divide backing into 2 (1¾-yard) lengths. Join panels lengthwise. Seam will run horizontally.

2. Layer backing, batting, and quilt top; baste. Quilt as desired. Quilt shown was outline quilted around diamonds, quilted in the ditch around blocks, and has large meandering in outer border *(Quilting Diagram)*.

3. Join (2¼"-wide) dark brown strips into 1 continuous piece for straight-grain French-fold binding. Add binding to quilt.

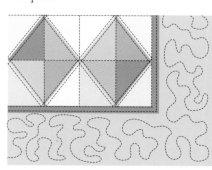

Quilting Diagram

SIZE OPTIONS

	Wallhanging (47" × 56")	Twin (67" × 95")	Queen (87" × 95")	King (107" × 108")
Blocks	9	30	42	63
Setting	3 × 3 blocks	5 × 6 blocks	7 × 6 blocks	9 × 7 blocks

MATERIALS

Assorted Light prints	6 fat eighths	10 fat quarters	14 fat quarters	21 fat quarters
Assorted Dark prints	6 fat eighths	10 fat quarters	14 fat quarters	21 fat quarters
Medium Brown print	¼ yard	⅜ yard	½ yard	½ yard
Dark Brown print	½ yard	⅝ yard	¾ yard	⅞ yard
Turquoise print	1⅜ yards	2 yards	2¼ yards	2⅝ yards
Backing Fabric	3 yards	5¾ yards	8 yards	9½ yards
Batting	Twin-size	Queen-size	Queen-size	King-size

From fat quarters, cut 2 (7½"-wide) strips. From strips, cut 6 (7½" × 6") rectangles.

TRIED & TRUE

We used fabrics from Moda's Madeira collection to create a cottage look.

 WEB EXTRA

Go to www.FonsandPorter.com/sdiamondsizes to download *Quilt Top Assembly Diagrams* for these size options.

DESIGNER

Quilt designer, teacher, and author Karla Alexander has been making quilts since she was a young girl. In 1998, she started the Saginaw Street Quilt Company, selling her ever-increasing and diverse pattern line. Her newest publication is *Stack the Deck Revisited*.

Kaleidoscope

Create the look of curves with simple straight-seam piecing. Stitching on paper foundations makes block construction easy!

PROJECT RATING: INTERMEDIATE
Size: 61½" × 77½"
Blocks: 48 (8") Kaleidoscope blocks

MATERIALS

20 fat quarters★ assorted light green and blue batiks
15 fat quarters★ assorted dark green and blue batiks
4 fat quarters★ assorted pink batiks
1 yard dark green batik for inner border and binding
1¼ yards teal batik for outer border
Fons & Porter Printed Foundation Papers or paper for foundations
4¾ yards backing fabric
Twin-size quilt batting
★fat quarter = 18" × 20"

Cutting

Pattern for foundation piecing is on page 121. Measurements include ¼" seam allowances. Border strips are exact length needed. You may want to make them longer to allow for piecing variations. For instructions on paper foundation piecing, see *Sew Easy: Paper Foundation Piecing* on page 123.

NOTE: Pieces are cut over-sized for foundation piecing.

From each light batik fat quarter, cut:
• 2 (5½"-wide) strips. From strips, cut 10 (5½" × 4") A rectangles.
• 1 (3¾") strip. From strip, cut 3 (3¾") squares. Cut squares in half to make 6 half-square B triangles.

From each dark batik fat quarter, cut:
• 2 (5½"-wide) strips. From strips, cut 10 (5½" × 4") A rectangles.
• 1 (3¾") strip. From strip, cut 3 (3¾") squares. Cut squares in half to make 6 half-square B triangles.

From each pink batik fat quarter, cut:
• 2 (5½"-wide) strips. From strips, cut 10 (5½" × 4") A rectangles.
• 1 (3¾") strip. From strip, cut 2 (3¾") squares. Cut squares in half to make 4 half-square B triangles.

From dark green batik, cut:
• 8 (2¼"-wide) strips for binding.

• 6 (1¾"-wide) strips. Piece strips to make 2 (1¾" × 64½") side inner borders and 2 (1¾" × 51") top and bottom inner borders.

From teal batik, cut:
• 7 (6"-wide) strips. Piece strips to make 2 (6" × 67") side outer borders and 2 (6" × 62") top and bottom outer borders.

Block Assembly

1. If not using Fons & Porter Printed Foundation Papers, trace 192 Block Segment Patterns (page 121) onto tracing paper. Roughly cut out patterns.

2. Referring to *Block Assembly Diagram* on page 120, foundation piece 4 block segments in numerical order, using pieces A and B as indicated. For detailed instructions, see *Sew Easy: Paper Foundation Piecing* on page 123.

3. Join 4 block segments as shown to complete 1 Block A. Make 18 Block A *(Block Diagrams* on page 120).

4. In the same manner, make 4 Block B, 6 Block C, 7 Block D, and 13 Block E.

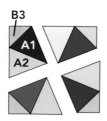

Block Assembly Diagram

Block A
Make 18

Block B
Make 4

Block C
Make 6

Block D
Make 7

Block E
Make 13

Block Diagrams

Quilt Top Assembly Diagram

Quilt Assembly

1. Lay out blocks as shown in *Quilt Top Assembly Diagram*.

2. Join into rows; join rows to complete quilt center.

3. Add dark green side inner borders to quilt center. Add top and bottom inner borders to quilt. Repeat for teal outer borders.

Finishing

1. Divide backing into 2 (2⅜-yard) lengths. Cut 1 piece in half lengthwise to make 2 narrow panels. Join 1 narrow panel to each side of wider panel; press seam allowances toward narrow panels.

2. Layer backing, batting, and quilt top; baste. Quilt as desired. Quilt shown was quilted in the ditch in blocks and has zigzag lines in the border *(Quilting Diagram)*.

3. Join (2¼"-wide) dark green batik strips into 1 continuous piece for straight-grain French-fold binding. Add binding to quilt.

Quilting Diagram

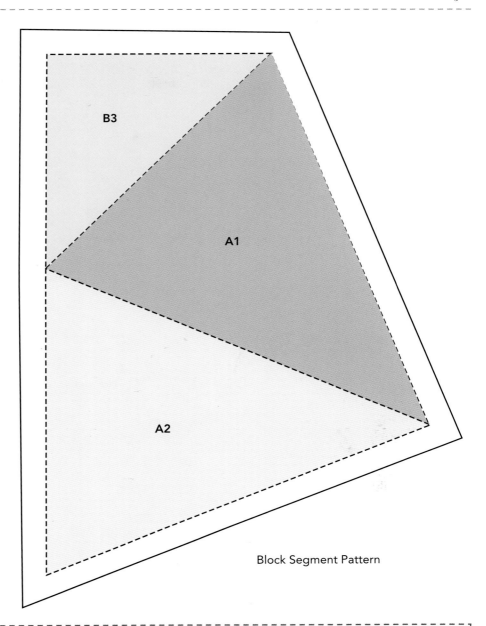

Block Segment Pattern

TRIED **&** TRUE

Pull fabrics from your stash of 1930s reproduction prints to make a charming Kaleidoscope variation.

DESIGNER

Gayle Brooks made her first quilt over thirty years ago, and hasn't stopped stitching since. She enjoys making quilts for her family and says she has more ideas than time!

Paper Foundation Piecing

Paper foundation piecing is ideal for small, intricate designs or designs with odd angles and sizes of pieces. Use this method for the blocks in *Kaleidoscope* on page 118. Eliminate tracing the patterns by using Fons & Porter's Printed Foundation Sheets.

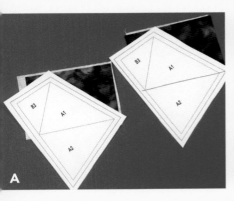

A

B

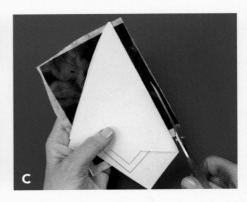

C

1. Using ruler and pencil, trace the outline of all shapes and the outer edge of the foundation pattern onto tracing paper. Number the pieces to indicate the stitching order. Using fabric pieces that are larger than the numbered areas, place fabrics for #1 and #2 right sides together. Position paper pattern atop fabrics with printed side of paper facing you *(Photo A)*. Make sure the fabric for #1 is under that area and that edges of fabrics extend ¼" beyond stitching line between the two sections.

2. Using a short machine stitch so papers will tear off easily later, stitch on line between the two areas, extending stitching into seam allowances at ends of seams.

3. Open out pieces and press or finger press the seam *(Photo B)*. The right sides of the fabric pieces will be facing out on the back side of the paper pattern.

4. Flip the work over and fold back paper pattern on stitched line. Trim seam allowance to ¼", being careful not to cut paper pattern *(Photo C)*.

5. Continue to add pieces in numerical order until pattern is covered. Use rotary cutter and ruler to trim excess paper and fabric along outer pattern lines.

6. Join pieced sections to complete block *(Photo D)*.

7. Carefully tear off foundation paper.

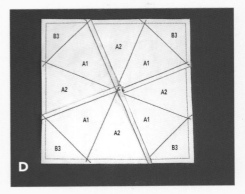

D

QUILT DESIGNED AND MADE BY **Dolores Smith and Sarah Maxwell.**
MACHINE QUILTED BY **Connie Gresham.**

Calicoes

Readers who have a passion for reproduction fabrics will love this quilt by Dolores Smith and Sarah Maxwell. Fabrics designed by Judie Rothermel are perfect for these traditional blocks.

PROJECT RATING: INTERMEDIATE

Size: 75¾" × 88½"

Blocks: 20 (9") Friendship Star blocks
30 (9") Churn Dash blocks

MATERIALS

NOTE: Fabrics in the quilt shown are from the Civil War Dressing Gowns II and Sturbridge Village Calico collections by Judie Rothermel for Marcus Fabrics.

4 fat quarters★ assorted red prints for blocks

½ yard each of 3 assorted gold prints for blocks

1⅜ yards light tan print for blocks

9 fat quarters★ assorted dark prints in green and blue for blocks and border

9 fat quarters★ assorted dark brown prints for blocks

15 fat quarters★ assorted medium prints in gray, tan, blue, and pink for blocks and border

¾ yard dark blue print for binding

5¼ yards backing fabric

Fons & Porter Half & Quarter Ruler (optional)

Full-size quilt batting

★fat quarter = 18" × 20"

Cutting

Measurements include ¼" seam allowances. Instructions are written for using the Fons & Porter Half & Quarter Ruler. If not using this ruler, follow cutting Notes. For instructions on using the Fons & Porter Half & Quarter Ruler, see *Sew Easy: Cutting Half-Square and Quarter-Square Triangles* on page 165.

From each red print, cut:

- 1 (3½"-wide) strip. From strip, cut 5 (3½") B squares.
- 3 (3½"-wide) strips. From strips, cut 20 half-square A triangles.
  NOTE: If NOT using the Fons & Porter Half & Quarter Ruler, cut 3 (3⅞"-wide) strips. From strips, cut 10 (3⅞") squares. Cut squares in half diagonally to make 20 half-square A triangles.

From each gold print, cut:

- 4 (3½"-wide) strips. From strips, cut 56 half-square A triangles.
  NOTE: If NOT using the Fons & Porter Half & Quarter Ruler, cut 3 (3⅞"-wide) strips. From strips, cut 28 (3⅞") squares. Cut squares in half diagonally to make 56 half-square A triangles.

From light tan print, cut:

- 13 (3½"-wide) strips. From strips, cut 200 half-square A triangles.
  NOTE: If NOT using the Fons & Porter Half & Quarter Ruler, cut 10 (3⅞"-wide) strips. From strips, cut 100 (3⅞") squares. Cut squares in half diagonally to make 200 half-square A triangles.

From each blue and green dark print, cut:

- 2 (3½"-wide) strips. From strips, cut 4 sets of 4 matching (3½" × 2") C rectangles.
- 2 (3½"-wide) strips. From strips, cut 4 sets of 4 matching half-square A triangles.
  NOTE: If NOT using the Fons & Porter Half & Quarter Ruler, cut 2 (3⅞"-wide) strips. From strips, cut 8 (3⅞") squares. Cut squares in half diagonally to make 4 sets of 4 matching half-square A triangles.

From each brown dark print, cut:

- 1 (3½"-wide) strip. From strip, cut 4 (3½") B squares.

From remaining blue, green, and brown dark prints, cut:

- 21 (3½"-wide) strips. From strips, cut a total of 104 (3½") B squares.

From each of 5 medium prints, cut:

- 1 (14"-wide) strip. From strip, cut 1 (14") square. Cut square in half diagonally in both directions to make 4 side setting triangles.

From each of 2 assorted medium prints, cut:

- 1 (7¼"-wide) strip. From strip, cut 1 (7¼") square. Cut square in half diagonally to make 2 corner setting triangles.

From remaining assorted medium prints, cut:

- 36 (3½"-wide) strips. From strips, cut 30 matching sets of 4 (3½" × 2") C rectangles and a total of 104 (3½") B squares.

From dark blue print, cut:

- 9 (2¼"-wide) strips for binding.

Friendship Star Block Assembly

1. Choose 1 set of 8 matching gold print A triangles, 4 matching red print A triangles and 1 B square, and 4 light tan print A triangles.
2. Join 1 gold print A triangle and 1 red print A triangle to make a triangle-square as shown in *Triangle-Square Diagrams*. Make 4 triangle-squares. In the same manner, make 4 triangle-squares using gold print and light tan print triangles.

Triangle-Square Diagrams

3. Lay out triangle-squares and red print B square as shown in *Friendship Star Block Assembly Diagram*. Join into rows; join rows to complete 1

Friendship Star block (*Friendship Star Block Diagram*). Make 20 Friendship Star blocks.

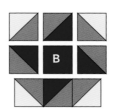 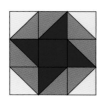

Friendship Star Block Assembly Diagram

Friendship Star Block Diagram

Churn Dash Block Assembly

1. Choose 1 set of 4 matching dark blue or green print A triangles and 4 C rectangles, 4 matching medium print C rectangles, 1 dark brown print B square, and 4 light tan print A triangles.
2. Make 4 triangle-squares using dark print and light tan print A triangles.
3. Join 1 dark print C rectangle and 1 medium print C rectangle as shown in *Rectangle Unit Diagrams*. Make 4 Rectangle Units.

Rectangle Unit Diagrams

4. Lay out triangle-squares, Rectangle Units, and dark brown print B square as shown in *Churn Dash Block Assembly Diagram*. Join into rows; join rows to complete 1 Churn Dash block (*Churn Dash Block Diagram*). Make 30 Churn Dash blocks.

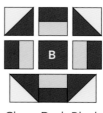 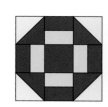

Churn Dash Block Assembly Diagram

Churn Dash Block Diagram

Quilt Top Assembly Diagram

Quilt Assembly

1. Lay out blocks and setting triangles as shown in *Quilt Top Assembly Diagram* on page 127. Join into diagonal rows; join rows to complete quilt center.

2. Referring to *Quilt Top Assembly Diagram* on page 127, lay out 22 assorted medium print B squares and 22 assorted dark print B squares as shown. Join squares to make top border. Repeat for bottom border.

3. In the same manner, join 30 assorted medium print B squares and 30 assorted dark print B squares to make 1 side border. Repeat for other side border.

4. Add top border to quilt center. Trim border even with edges of quilt center if necessary. Repeat for bottom border.

5. In the same manner, add side borders to quilt.

> ### Sew **Smart**™
> Instead of trimming side borders to fit, adjust a few seam allowances to make borders fit and make seams in corners match. —Liz

Finishing

1. Divide backing into 2 (2⅝ -yard) lengths. Cut 1 piece in half lengthwise to make 2 narrow panels. Join 1 narrow panel to each side of wider panel; press seam allowances toward narrow panels.

2. Layer backing, batting, and quilt top; baste. Quilt as desired. Quilt shown was quilted with a Celtic knot design *(Quilting Diagram)*.

3. Join 2¼"-wide dark blue print strips into 1 continuous piece for straight-grain French-fold binding. Add binding to quilt.

	Crib (37½" × 50¼")	Queen/King (101¼" × 101¼")
Friendship Star Blocks	2	36
Churn Dash Blocks	6	49

MATERIALS

	Crib	Queen/King
Red Prints	2 fat eighths	8 fat quarters
Gold Prints	2 fat eighths	¾ yard each of 3
Light Tan Print	1 fat quarter	2 yards
Assorted Dark Blue and Green Prints	6 fat eighths	14 fat quarters
Dark Brown Prints	6 fat eighths	7 fat quarters
Assorted Medium Prints	9 fat quarters	16 fat quarters
Dark Blue Print	½ yard	1 yard
Backing Fabric	1½ yards	9 yards
Batting	Crib-size	King-size

WEB EXTRA

Go to www.FonsandPorter.com/calicoessizes to download *Quilt Top Assembly Diagrams* for these size options.

Quilting Diagram

DESIGNERS

Sarah Maxwell and Dolores Smith, owners of Homestead Hearth™ pattern company, have a passion for creating original patterns using many prints from their stash or from a single fabric line. ✳

> **TRIED & TRUE**
>
> We used fabrics from Elm Creek Quilts: The Quilters Kitchen Collection by Jennifer Chiaverini for Red Rooster Fabrics for the sample blocks shown.
>
>

Brave New World

This fun patchwork quilt uses just one simple unit which can be arranged in a variety of ways.
See our alternate setting suggestions on page 133.

PROJECT RATING: INTERMEDIATE
Size: 60" × 92"
Blocks: 15 (16") blocks

MATERIALS

20 fat quarters★★ assorted dark prints in blue, green, gold, orange, and brown for blocks and outer border

5 fat quarters★★ assorted red prints for blocks and borders

20 fat eighths★ assorted light prints for blocks and outer border

⅝ yard dark red print for binding

5½ yards backing fabric

Full-size quilt batting

★fat eighth = 9" × 20"

★★fat quarter = 18" × 20"

Cutting

Measurements include ¼" seam allowances. Border strips are exact length needed. You may want to make them longer to allow for piecing variations.

From each dark print fat quarter, cut:

• 2 (4⅞"-wide) strips. From strips, cut 7 (4⅞") squares. Cut squares in half diagonally to make 14 half-square B triangles. (You will have a few extra.)
• 2 (2½"-wide) strips. From strips, cut 14 (2½") A squares. (You will have a few extra.)

From each red fat quarter, cut:

• 1 (4⅞"-wide) strip. From strip, cut 4 (4⅞") squares. Cut squares in half diagonally to make 8 half-square B triangles.
• 1 (2½"-wide) strip. From strip, cut 8 (2½") A squares.
• 3 (2½"-wide) strips. Piece strips to make 2 (2½" × 80½") side inner borders and 2 (2½" × 52½") top and bottom inner borders.

From each light print fat eighth, cut:

• 3 (2⅞"-wide) strips. From strips, cut 16 (2⅞") squares and 1 (2½") A square. Cut (2⅞") squares in half diagonally to make 32 half-square C triangles. (You will have a few extra.)

From dark red print, cut:

• 8 (2¼"-wide) strips for binding.

Block Assembly

1. Referring to *Brave New World Diagrams*, lay out 1 dark A square, 2 light C triangles, and 1 dark B triangle. Join to make one Brave New World Unit. Repeat to make 308 Units. See *Sew Easy: Trimming Triangles* on page 133 to learn how to trim points for more accurate piecing.

Brave New World Diagrams

2. Referring to *Block Assembly Diagram* on page 132, lay out 16 Brave New World Units as shown. Join into quadrants; join quadrants to complete 1 block (*Block Diagram*). Make 15 blocks.

Quilt Assembly

1. Referring to *Quilt Top Assembly Diagram* on page 132, lay out blocks as shown. Join into rows; join rows to complete quilt center.

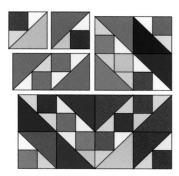

Block Assembly Diagram

Block Diagram

Quilt Top Assembly Diagram

2. Add side inner borders to quilt center. Add top and bottom inner borders to quilt.

3. Referring to *Quilt Top Assembly Diagram,* join 20 Brave New World Units for side outer border. Join 1 light A square and 1 dark A square; add to end of border. Repeat for opposite end of border to complete 1 side outer border. Make 2 side outer borders. Add borders to quilt.

4. In the same manner, join 14 Brave New World Units and 2 pairs of A square spacers to make top border. Repeat for bottom border. Add borders to quilt.

Finishing

1. Divide backing fabric into 2 (2¾-yard) pieces. Cut 1 piece in half lengthwise to make 2 narrow panels. Join 1 narrow panel to each side of wider panel; press seam allowances toward narrow panels.

2. Layer backing, batting, and quilt top; baste. Quilt as desired. Quilt shown is utility quilted using size 8 perle cotton.

3. Join 2¼"-wide red print strips into 1 continuous piece for straight-grain French-fold binding. Add binding to quilt.

Trimming Triangles

The Fons & Porter Triangle Trimmers will make piecing Brave New World Units easy and accurate.

A **B**

1. With right sides facing, lay 1 light triangle atop a square, aligning square corners. The triangle tip extends beyond the square. Lay each triangle trimmer atop the triangle to see which is the right one to trim triangle tip even with the square. To fit triangle exactly to the square, use the pink trimmer to trim the tip perpendicular to the short side of the triangle *(Photo A)*. Stitch the triangle to one side of the square as shown.

2. Open out triangle and press seam allowances toward triangle. With right sides facing, lay the second triangle atop the joined pieces. Again lay each triangle trimmer atop pieces to determine which will trim the triangle tip to exactly fit the stitched pieces. Use the blue trimmer to trim tip perpendicular to long side of triangle *(Photo B)*. Join the triangle to the adjacent side of square. Open out triangle; press seam allowances toward triangle.

More Setting Options

The Simple Cross

This quilt is ideal for using scraps and works well for a Cutting Bee (see page 162) or fabric strip exchange. If you tend to collect more dark and medium prints than light ones, this pattern will make good use of what you have on hand. The large blocks go together quickly to make a bed quilt.

PROJECT RATING: EASY
Finished Size: 100" × 100"
Blocks: 36 (12") Simple Cross blocks

MATERIALS

- 80 (2½"-wide) strips assorted medium/dark prints for blocks and sashing
- 22 (2½"-wide) strips assorted light prints for blocks and sashing
- 4 (4½"-wide) strips assorted light prints for blocks
- 1¼ yards dark brown print for inner border and binding
- 3 yards medium brown print for outer border
- 9 yards backing fabric
- King-size quilt batting

Cutting

Measurements include ¼" seam allowances. Cut crosswise strips unless otherwise noted. Border strips are exact length needed. You may want to cut them longer to allow for piecing variations.

From 2½"-wide assorted medium/dark print strips, cut a total of:
- 84 (2½" × 12½") sashing strips.
- 144 (2½" × 8½") D rectangles.
- 144 (2½" × 4½") C rectangles.

From 2½"-wide assorted light print strips, cut a total of:
- 288 (2½") B squares.
- 49 (2½") sashing squares.

From 4½"-wide assorted light print strips, cut a total of:
- 36 (4½") A squares.

From dark brown print, cut:
- 9 (1½"-wide) strips. Piece strips to make 2 (1½" × 88½") top and bottom inner borders and 2 (1½" × 86½") side inner borders.
- 10 (2¼"-wide) strips for binding.

From medium brown print, cut:
- 4 (6½"-wide) **lengthwise** strips for borders. From strips, cut 2 (6½" × 100½") top and bottom outer borders and 2 (6½" × 88½") side outer borders.

Block Assembly

1. Select 1 A square, 8 B squares, 4 C rectangles, and 4 D rectangles.
2. Lay out squares and rectangles as shown in *Block Assembly Diagram*. Join into sections; join sections to compete 1 Simple Cross block (*Block Diagram*).
3. Make 36 Simple Cross blocks.

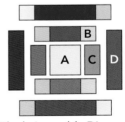

Block Assembly Diagram

Block Diagram

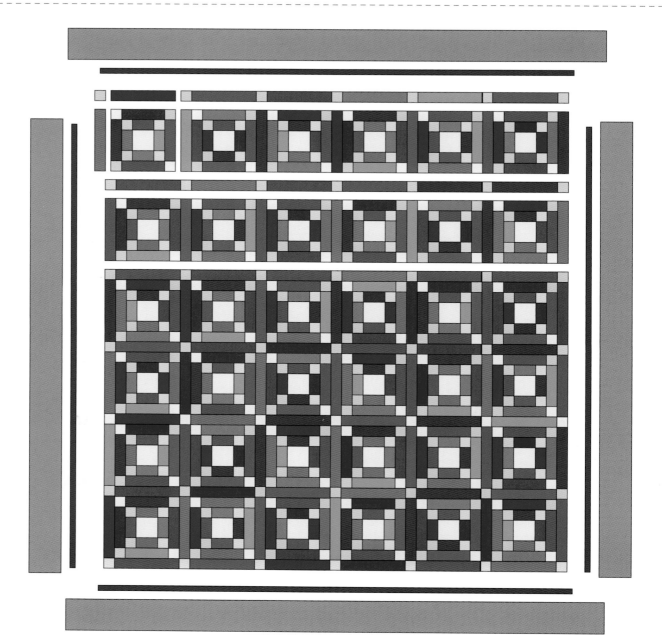

Quilt Top Assembly Diagram

Quilt Assembly

1. Lay out blocks, sashing strips, and B squares as shown in *Quilt Top Assembly Diagram*. Join into rows; join rows to complete quilt center.

2. Add dark brown print side inner borders to quilt center. Add dark brown print top and bottom inner borders to quilt.

3. Repeat for medium brown print outer borders.

Finishing

1. Divide backing into 3 (3-yard) lengths. Join panels lengthwise.

2. Layer backing, batting, and quilt top; baste. Quilt as desired. Quilt shown was machine-quilted with an allover leaf pattern.

3. Join 2¼"-wide dark brown strips into 1 continuous piece for straight-grain French-fold binding. Add binding to quilt.

Sew **Smart**™
I find it tedious to piece skinny sashing rows, so I came up with a way to add sashing as I go. See *Sew Easy: Pre-Sashing Blocks for Quicker Setting* on page 29 to learn this technique. —Liz

TRIED & TRUE

The square in the center of the Simple Cross block is ideal for signatures. For this quilt, each member of the magazine team made a block and signed the center. Some people stamped or embellished their blocks. We used one color for the light fabric and another color for the sashing strips, and made the blocks scrappy.

DESIGNER

Lauren Caswell Brooks is a former features editor of *Fons & Porter's Love of Quilting*. A native of Alpharetta, Georgia, Lauren lives in Birmingham, Alabama, with her husband, Joel. She graduated from the University of Georgia with a degree in journalism.

Jacob's Ladder

Because you need both light and dark fabrics for this quilt, it's a great Cutting Bee project (see page 162). The popular Bible-themed pattern uses the placement of contrasting fabrics to create the illusion of stairs. The large light-colored squares symbolize the windows of heaven.

PROJECT RATING: EASY
Finished Size: 84" × 84"
Blocks: 36 (12") Jacob's Ladder blocks

MATERIALS

- 18 (2½"-wide) strips assorted medium/dark prints for blocks
- 11 (4½"-wide) strips assorted medium/dark prints for blocks
- 19 (2½"-wide) strips assorted light prints for blocks and borders
- 23 (4½"-wide) strips assorted light prints for blocks and borders
- 1¼ yards red print for inner border and binding
- Fons & Porter Half & Quarter Ruler
- 7½ yards backing fabric
- Queen-size quilt batting

Cutting

Measurements include ¼" seam allowances. Instructions are written for using the Fons & Porter Half & Quarter Ruler. See *Sew Easy: Cutting Half-Square and Quarter-Square Triangles* on page 165.

From 2½"-wide assorted medium/dark print strips, cut a total of:
- 288 (2½") squares.

From 4½"-wide assorted medium/dark print strips, cut a total of:
- 152 half-square triangles.

From 2½"-wide assorted light print strips, cut a total of:
- 292 (2½") squares.

From 4½"-wide strips assorted light prints, cut:
- 152 half-square triangles.
- 108 (4½") squares.

From red print, cut:
- 8 (2½"-wide) strips. Piece strips to make 4 (2½" × 72½") outer borders.
- 9 (2¼"-wide) strips for binding.

Block Assembly

1. Join 2 light print and 2 dark print 2½" squares as shown in *Four-Patch Unit Diagrams*. Make 144 Four Patch Units.

Four Patch Unit Diagrams

2. Join 1 light print half-square triangle and 1 dark print half-square triangle as shown in Triangle-Square Diagrams. Make 152 triangle-squares.

Triangle-Square Diagrams

3. Lay out 5 Four Patch Units and 4 triangle-squares as shown in *Block A Assembly Diagram*. Join into rows; join rows to complete 1 Block A *(Block Diagrams)*.

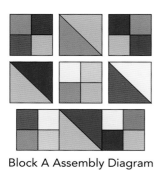

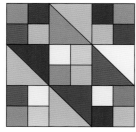

Block A Assembly Diagram

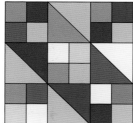

Block A
Make 4

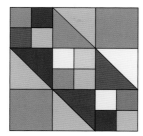

Block B
Make 4

Block C
Make 12

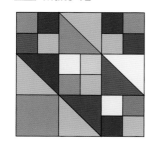

Block D
Make 16

Block Diagrams

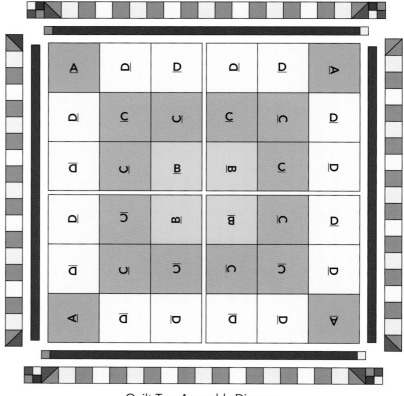

Quilt Top Assembly Diagram

4. In the same manner, make 4 Block B.

5. Make 12 Block C and 16 Block D using Four Patch Units, triangle-squares, and 4½" squares as shown.

Quilt Assembly

1. Referring to photo on page 141 and *Quilt Top Assembly Diagram,* lay out blocks as shown. Join into rows; join rows to complete quilt center.

2. Add 1 red print inner side border to each side of quilt center.

3. Add 1 light print 2½" square to each end of remaining inner borders. Add borders to top and bottom of quilt.

4. Join 17 (4½") light print squares and 2 triangle-squares to make 1 outer border. Make 4 outer borders.

5. Add 1 pieced outer border to each side of quilt. Add 1 Four Patch Unit

to each end of remaining pieced borders. Add borders to top and bottom of quilt.

Finishing

1. Divide backing into 3 (2½-yard) lengths. Cut 1 piece in half lengthwise to make 2 narrow panels. Join 1 narrow panel to 2 wider panels. Remaining narrow panel is extra and can be used to make a hanging sleeve.

2. Layer backing, batting, and quilt top; baste. Quilt as desired. Quilt shown was quilted with an allover leaf pattern.

3. Join 2¼"-wide red print strips into 1 continuous piece for straight-grain French-fold binding. Add binding to quilt.

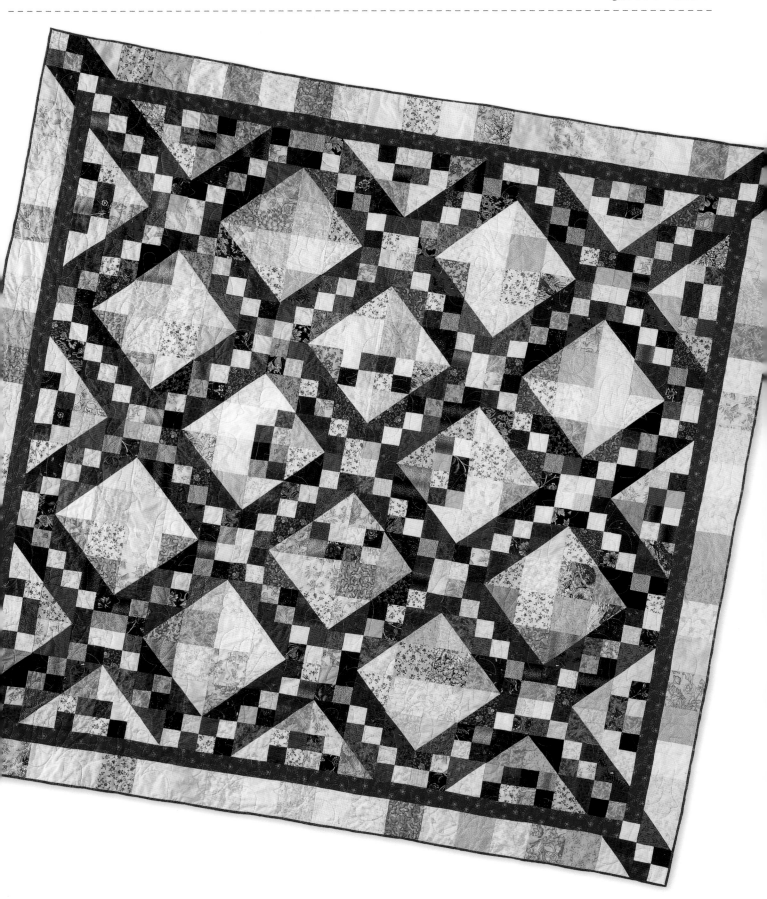

Flock of Geese

A beautiful way to use a collection of fat quarters, this Flock of Geese quilt presents a pleasing medley of colors. Rather than putting the triangles in traditional straight rows, we clustered them for a refreshing, new look.

PROJECT RATING: INTERMEDIATE
Finished Size: 60" × 76"
Blocks: 12 (16") Flock of Geese blocks

MATERIALS

Note: This quilt uses 20"-long strips.
40 (2½" × 20") strips assorted medium/dark prints for blocks and pieced borders
16 (4½" × 20") strips assorted medium/dark prints for blocks and pieced borders
40 (2½" × 20") strips assorted light prints for blocks and pieced borders
16 (4½" × 20") strips assorted light prints for blocks and pieced borders
¾ yard navy print for inner border
¾ yard dark print for binding
Fons & Porter Half & Quarter Ruler
4 yards backing fabric
Twin-size quilt batting

Cutting

Measurements include ¼" seam allowances. Instructions are written for using the Fons & Porter Half & Quarter Ruler. See *Sew Easy: Cutting Half-Square and Quarter-Square Triangles* on page 165.

Stack 2½"-wide medium/dark and light strips, right sides facing. Cut:

• 512 half-square A triangle pairs.

Stack 4½"-wide medium/dark and light strips, right sides facing. Cut:

• 128 half-square B triangle pairs.

From navy print, cut:

• 8 (2½"-wide) strips. Piece strips to make 2 (2½" × 64½") side inner borders and 2 (2½" × 52½") top and bottom inner borders.

From dark print, cut:

• 8 (2¼"-wide) strips for binding.

Unit Assembly

1. Join 1 light print A triangle and 1 dark print A triangle as shown in *Triangle-Square Diagrams*. Make 512 small triangle-squares.

Triangle-Square Diagrams

2. In the same manner, join 1 light print B triangle and 1 dark print B triangle to make 1 large triangle-square. Make 128 large triangle squares.

3. Referring to *Cluster Diagrams*, join 4 small triangle-squares as shown. Make 124 Clusters.

Cluster Diagrams

Block Assembly

1. Referring to *Quadrant Diagrams*, lay out 2 large triangle-squares and 2 Clusters as shown. Join into rows; join rows to complete 1 Quadrant. Make 48 Quadrants.

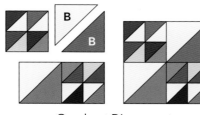

Quadrant Diagrams

2. Lay out 4 quadrants as shown in *Block Diagram*. Join quadrants into rows; join rows to complete 1 block. Make 12 blocks.

Block Diagram

Border Assembly

1. Referring to *Border Unit Diagrams*, join pairs of large triangle-squares to make 14 Border Unit 1.

2. Join pairs of Clusters to make 10 Border Unit 2.

3. Referring to *Border Unit Diagrams*, join Clusters and small triangle-squares to make 4 each of Border Unit 3 and Border Unit 4.

4. Referring to *Quilt Top Assembly Diagram*, join 4 Border Unit 1, 3 Border Unit 2, 1 Border Unit 3, and 1 Border Unit 4 as shown to make pieced side outer border. Make 2 pieced side outer borders.

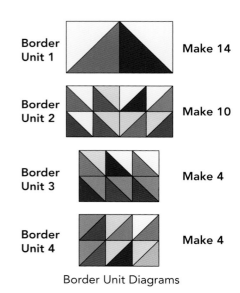

Border Unit Diagrams

5 In a similar manner, make pieced top outer border. Repeat for pieced bottom outer border.

Quilt Assembly

1. Lay out blocks as shown in *Quilt Top Assembly Diagram*. Join blocks into rows; join rows to complete quilt center.

2. Add navy print side inner borders to quilt center. Add navy print top and bottom inner borders to quilt.

3. Repeat for pieced outer borders.

Finishing

1. Divide backing into 2 (2-yard) lengths. Join panels lengthwise. Seam will run horizontally.

2. Layer backing, batting, and quilt top; baste. Quilt as desired. Quilt shown was outline-quilted.

3. Join 2¼"-wide dark print strips into 1 continuous piece to make straight-grain French-fold binding. Add binding to quilt.

Quilt Top Assembly Diagram

TRIED & TRUE

A monotone color scheme of cool blues works well with this block. Note that even with a uniform color, the fabrics are scrappy enough to create visual interest.

Antique Baby Blocks

Liz and Marianne discovered this unusual old quilt, in what appears to be an original version of the Baby Blocks design, in an antique shop in Vermont. The colors and fabrics suggest the quilt was made around 1870.

PROJECT RATING: CHALLENGING
Size: 69¼" × 67½"
Blocks: 23 Baby Blocks cubes

MATERIALS

45 fat eighths★ assorted light/ medium/dark prints in brown, rust, gold, and pink for blocks. (Use additional fabrics for more variety.)
2½ yards light print for setting pieces and binding
4 yards backing fabric
Twin-size quilt batting
Template material
★fat eighth = 9" × 20"

Cutting

Measurements include ¼" seam allowances. Make templates from patterns A and B on page 148.

From each fat eighth, cut:
• 3 (2½"-wide) strips for diamond strip sets.

From light print, cut:
• 21 (2⅞"-wide) strips. From strips, cut: 60 (2⅞" × 7½") C setting rectangles, 22 A pieces, and 10 B triangles.
• 8 (2¼"-wide) strips for binding.

Block Assembly

Note: See *Sew Easy: Working with 60-degree Diamonds* on page 150 for helpful tips on making the strip sets, joining rows of diamonds, and piecing a cube.

1. Join 3 (2½"-wide) strips to make 1 strip set, offsetting ends by approximately 1½". Make 45 strip sets.
2. From strip sets, cut 267 (2½"-wide) 60-degree diamond rows, using marking on ruler.

3. Choose 3 diamond rows. Join to make 1 large, pieced diamond. Make 89 large diamonds.
4. Lay out 3 diamonds to form cube. Join to make 1 Baby Block cube. Make 23 Baby Block cubes. Remaining large diamonds are for sides and top and bottom edges.
5. Referring to *Quilt Top Assembly Diagram* on page 149, join 2 diamonds as shown to make 1 Right Side Unit. Make 2 Right and 2 Left Side Units.

Quilt Assembly

1. Lay out Baby Block cubes and setting pieces as shown in *Quilt Top Assembly Diagram on page 149.*
2. Join C rectangles to lower edges of cubes and side units. Join into rows, alternating cubes with A setting pieces.
3. Set B triangles into openings between setting rectangles on bottom row of cubes. Set large pieced diamonds into openings along bottom row of cubes as shown.

4. To make top row, join C setting
rectangles to bottom edges of large
diamonds as shown. Join setting rectangles using B triangles.

5. Join rows, setting in pieces.

6. Trim edges of quilt even with edges
of cubes on sides and even with edges
of B triangles on top and bottom.

Quilting and Finishing

1. Divide backing fabric into 2
(2-yard) lengths. Cut 1 piece in half
lengthwise to make 2 narrow panels.
Join 1 narrow panel to each side of
wider panel; press seam allowances
toward narrow panels.

2. Layer backing, batting, and quilt top;
baste. Quilt as desired. Quilt shown
was hand quilted in the ditch around
all pieces.

3. Join 2¼"-wide light print strips
into 1 continuous piece for
straight-grain French-fold
binding. Add binding
to quilt. ✳

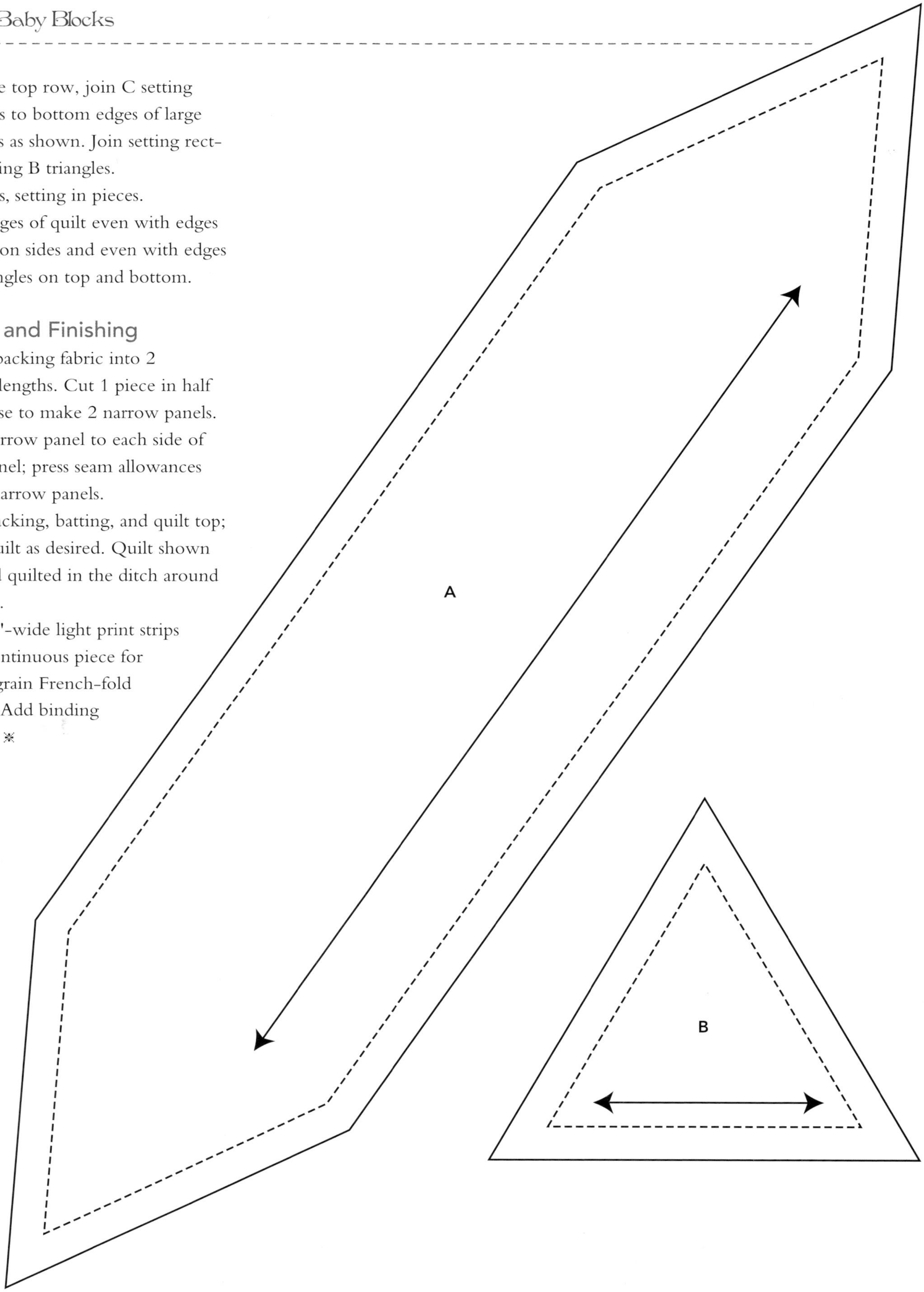

A

B

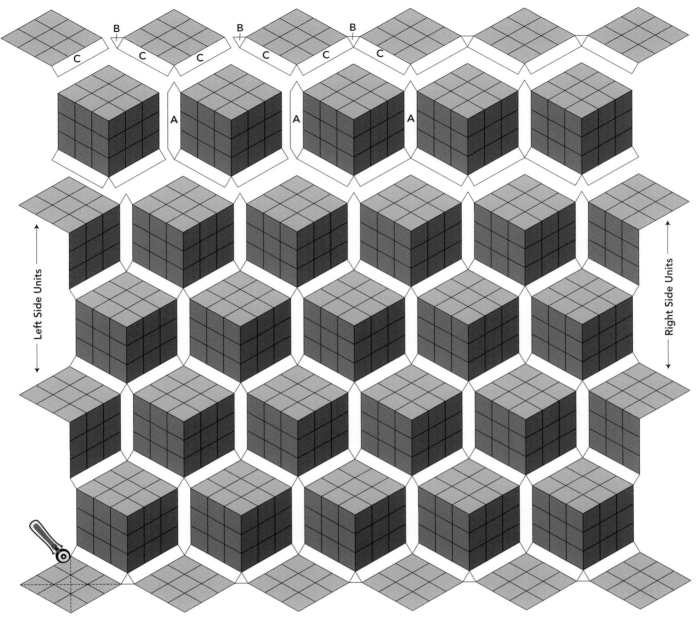

Quilt Top Assembly Diagram

Sew Easy™
Working with 60° Diamonds

Single diamonds and groups of diamonds joined into a strip set are easy to cut with a rotary cutter and ruler with 60° angle markings. Once you've cut the diamonds, follow our easy instructions to join rows of diamonds into larger pieced diamonds, and then diamond cubes.

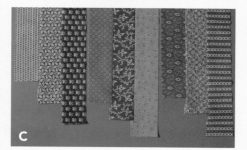

Cutting Single Diamonds

1. Begin by cutting a strip of desired width. Align the 60-degree angle mark on your ruler with 1 long edge of strip. Cut along edge of ruler, trimming end of strip at a 60-degree angle (*Photo A*).
2. Turn the trimmed strip and align the 60-degree guide on ruler with 1 long edge of strip and the 2½" strip width guide on ruler with angled cut edge. Cut along ruler to cut 1 diamond (*Photo B*).

Making Large, Pieced Diamonds

1. For the Antique Baby Blocks quilt on page 146, small diamonds are arranged in 3 rows of 3 diamonds each to make the large pieced diamonds. Begin by cutting 1 (2½"-wide) strip each of 9 different fabrics for the small diamonds. Join strips into 3 strip sets with 3 strips in each strip set, off-setting strips at one end by approximately 1½" (*Photo C*). Press seam allowances to one side.
2. Align 60-degree angle cutting guide on ruler with long edge of strip set. Cut along edge of ruler (*Photo D*).
3. Align 60-degree guide on ruler with one long edge of strip set and 2½" strip width guide on ruler with angled cut edge. Cut along ruler to cut 1 (3-diamond) row (*Photo E*). Cut desired number of 3-diamond rows from strip set. Repeat to cut 3-diamond rows from other 2 strip sets.
4. Lay out 3-diamond rows as shown in *Photo F*. Join rows to make large diamond, matching diamond seams ¼" from raw edge as shown in *Photo G*.
5. If diamonds do not match, give them the "pinch test" by pinching a slightly deeper seam with your fingers. If the alignment becomes worse (*Photo H*), your seam was too wide. You will need to pick out the part of the seam where diamonds meet and restitch with a slightly narrower seam. If the alignment improves with pinching, restitch with a slightly wider seam at diamond intersections.

Making a Cube

1. To prepare to make a cube as shown in *Photo I*, choose fabrics for 2 more large diamonds. Cut strips, join into strip sets, and cut 3-diamond rows as directed in steps #1– #3. Join 3-diamond rows into large diamonds.

E

F

G

H

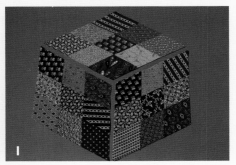

I

2. Pin left and right diamonds together, aligning small diamond seams. To secure seam without stitching in reverse, position large diamonds "backwards" in sewing machine (*Photo J*). Sew forward to the beginning point of seam (¼" from raw edge) and pivot with needle down.

3. Sew forward, taking ¼" seam (*Photo K*). Stop stitching ¼" from end of diamonds, pivot so work is again "backwards" in the sewing machine, and sew forward a few stitches to secure end of seam. The seam allowances at the beginning and end of the seam should be free to allow for setting in pieces.

4. Set top large diamond into opening between left and right large diamonds. Pin top diamond to 1 side diamond and stitch seam (*Photo L*). Start and stop stitching ¼" from ends of seams as before to allow for setting in pieces.

5. Pin top large diamond to the other side diamond, matching small diamond seams (*Photo M*). Join diamonds to complete cube (*Photo N*), leaving ends of seams free.

J

K

L

M

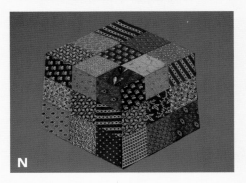

N

Katie's String Star

"To me, string quilts are the ultimate scrap quilts," says designer Katie Porter. "Assorted fabric strips too small to use for other projects are perfect for these quilts. Try my quick-and-easy method for making this quilt that is much easier to make than it looks."

PROJECT RATING: INTERMEDIATE

Size: 86" × 98"

MATERIALS

5 yards dark blue print for setting diamonds, borders, and binding

⅝ yard red print for inner border

25 (¼-yard pieces) assorted light, medium, and dark prints for string stars

Fons & Porter's 60° Pyramids Ruler or template material

Fons & Porter's 60° Diamonds Ruler or template material

7⅞ yards backing fabric

Queen-size quilt batting

Cutting

If you are not using Fons & Porter's 60° Pyramids and Fons & Porter's 60° Diamonds rulers, make templates from the patterns on pages 154 and 157. Measurements include ¼" seam allowances. Border strips are exact length needed. You may want to make them longer to allow for piecing variations.

From dark blue print, cut:

- 11 (5¾"-wide) strips. From strips, cut 55 (5¾") A diamonds. (See *Sew Easy: Cutting 60° Diamonds and Pyramids* on page 113 for instructions to cut diamonds.)

- 3 (5¾"-wide) strips. From strips, cut 6 (5¾" × 18⅞") rectangles. Trim both ends of rectangles at 60-degree angle to make C trapezoids *(Trapezoid Cutting Diagrams on page 154)*.

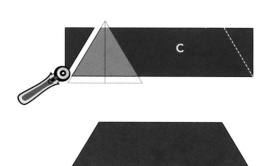

Trapezoid Cutting Diagrams

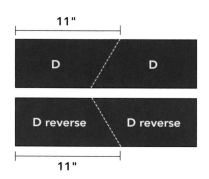

Half Trapezoid Cutting Diagrams

Strip Set Diagram

2. Referring to *Sew Easy: Cutting 60° Diamonds and Pyramids* on page 113, cut 248 B triangles from strip sets.

Quilt Assembly

1. Referring to *Quilt Top Assembly Diagram*, join 4 B triangles, 3 C trapezoids, and 1 D and 1 D reverse half trapezoid to complete Row 1.

2. In a similar manner, lay out A diamonds and B triangles as shown in Row 2. Join pieces into diagonal segments; join segments to complete Row 2.

3. Continue making rows as shown. When all horizontal rows are completed, join rows to complete quilt center. Straighten sides of quilt by trimming ¼" outside star points.

• 1 (5¾"-wide) strip. From strip, cut 2 (5¾" × 18½") rectangles. Referring to *Half Trapezoid Cutting Diagrams*, measure 11" from top left corner and cut strip at a 60-degree angle to make 2 D half trapezoids. In a similar manner, measure 11" from bottom left corner and cut 2 D reverse half trapezoids.

• 9 (6"-wide) strips. Piece strips to make 2 (6" × 87½") side outer borders and 2 (6" × 86½") top and bottom outer borders.

• 10 (2¼"-wide) strips for binding.

From red print, cut:

• 9 (2"-wide) strips. Piece strips to make 2 (2" × 84½") side inner borders and 2 (2" × 75½") top and bottom inner borders.

From each ¼-yard piece, cut:

• 5 crosswise strips ranging in width from 1¼"–2¼" for strip sets.

Cutting Triangles

1. Referring to *Strip Set Diagram*, join strips randomly by color and width into strip sets at least 6" wide. Make 25 strip sets.

B

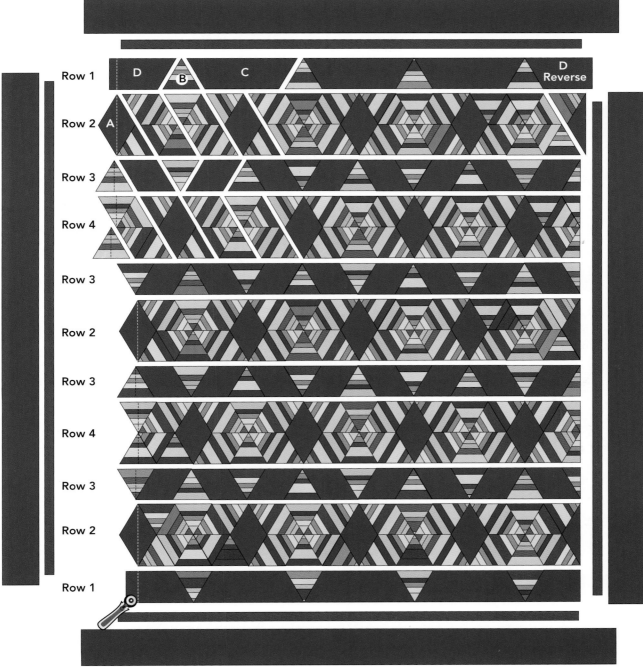

Row 1 D B C D Reverse

Row 2 A

Row 3

Row 4

Row 3

Row 2

Row 3

Row 4

Row 3

Row 2

Row 1

Quilt Top Assembly Diagram

4. Add red print side inner borders to quilt center. Add top and bottom inner borders to quilt.

5. Repeat for dark blue outer borders.

Quilting and Finishing

1. Divide backing fabric into 3 (2⅝-yard) pieces. Join pieces lengthwise. Seams will run horizontally.

2. Layer backing, batting, and quilt top; baste. Quilt as desired. Quilt shown was quilted with concentric diamonds

in the diamonds, in the ditch on the stars, and with a rope design in the border.

3. Join 2¼"-wide dark blue print strips into 1 continuous piece for straight-grain French-fold binding. Add binding to quilt.

DESIGNER

Katie Porter, daughter of Liz Porter, has been quilting since she was sixteen years old. She is a frequent contributor to *Love of Quilting* magazine. Katie is an attorney who loves to try all kinds of quilting in her spare time. ✳

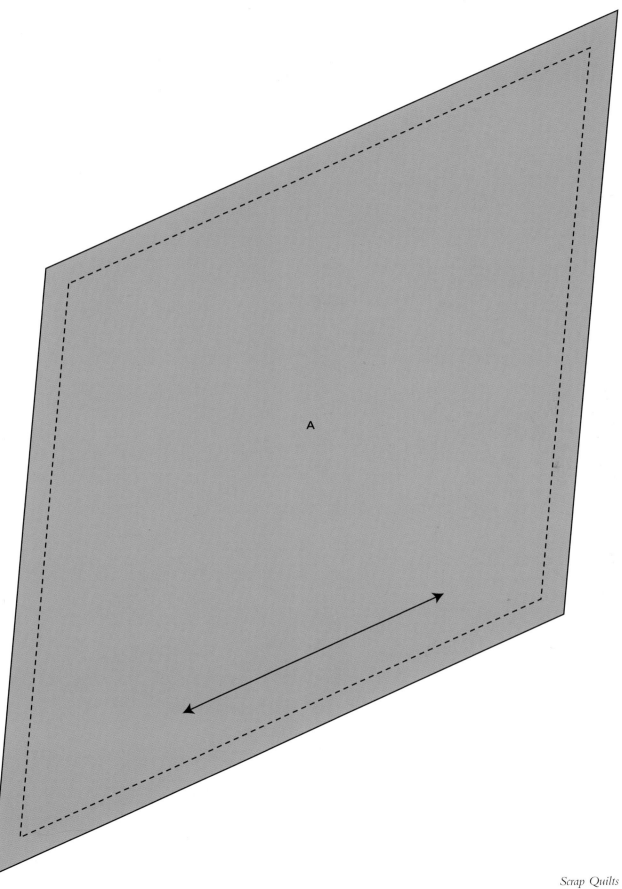

A

Cathedral Window

This Cathedral Window technique involves no batting, backing, or binding. The three-dimensional effect is achieved by folding squares of fabric and stitching smaller squares of contrasting fabric under the folds. The overall effect is that of brilliant stained-glass windows. For a scrappy version, see page 161.

Before Beginning

Instructions below are for making one 4-unit Cathedral Window section. A bed-size quilt requres a lot of muslin—usually about 30 yards. To make sure the fabric is consistent throughout your quilt, buy the required amount at once. We suggest you practice this technique by making one 4–unit section before purchasing extensive yardage.

1 (4–unit Section): 6¾" square

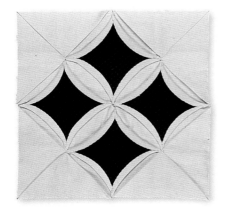

Block Assembly

Note: We used contrasting thread in photography for clarity; you will want to use matching thread.

1. Fold 1 muslin square in half and press. Stitch ¼" seam across each short end *(Photo A)*.

A

2. Pull unsewn edges apart and flatten unit into square so that sewn edges meet at center. Press unit so that corners are crisp and square and seams are pressed in opposite directions *(Photo B)*.

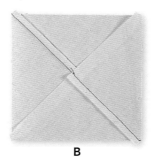

B

3. Sew remaining raw edges together with ¼" seam from corner to corner to just past center seam. Then sew from opposite corner just far enough to leave 1" opening (see arrow in *Photo C*).

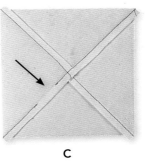

C

4. Turn square right side out through opening and press flat *(Photo D)*. Unit will be approximately 4¾" square.

D

5. Working with seam side of unit facing up, fold each corner to center and pin; press fold to form guidelines for stitching *(Photo E)*.

6. Repeat steps #1–#5 to make 3 more units.

E

7. Place 2 units together with unseamed sides facing, aligning corners carefully. Stitch unit together on folded guidelines to make row *(Photo F)*. Make 2 (2-unit) rows.

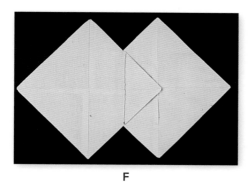

F

8. Join rows together in same manner to make 1 (4-unit) section. Once rows are joined, hand tack loose corners at center of each unit *(Photo G)*.

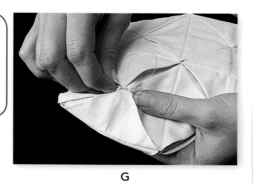

G

9. Place 2" fabric square over seam that joins units *(Photo H)*.

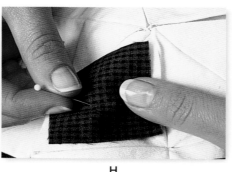

H

10. Roll folded muslin edges over raw edges of insert and blindstitch in place, sewing through all layers *(Photo I)*. Taper muslin at corners. Repeat with remaining inserts to complete section.

I

11. Make required number of sections. Stitch sections together on folded guidelines. Place 2" fabric squares in place over seams and blindstitch muslin over raw edges.

12. Finish edge by adding triangular windows in frames or just stitch the muslin down with no fabric inside.

Approximate Muslin Yardage Chart

Quilt Size	45"-wide muslin	90"-wide muslin	Approximate Units Needed
Crib (30" × 45")	9 yards	4 yards	140
Twin (60" × 80")	21 yards	9 yards	450
Double/Full (80" × 95")	26 yards	12 yards	715
Queen (86" × 100")	30 yards	15 yards	806
King (106" × 106")	35 yards	18 yards	1,024

Eugenia L. Hardin made this scrappy version of Cathedral Window—a popular option among fabric collectors.

DESIGNER

Fleda Collins is a retired teacher from Talbott, Tennessee. "Since my husband, Felix, and I travel a lot, the Cathedral Window was a great take-along project," says Fleda. The quilt won first place at the Rose Center Quilt Show and third place in the Dogwood Arts Festival in Knoxville, Tennessee.✻

Cutting Bees are the Latest Buzz

A Cutting Bee is a modern version of the old-fashioned quilting bee. Instead of joining forces around a frame to get a top quilted for one person, the participants gather at tables with rotary cutters, mats, and rulers to get a quilt started for each person. Each quilter brings a big pile of fabrics in an agreed-upon color scheme, cutting tools, and something good to eat.

The idea of a Cutting Bee is to benefit everyone involved by getting a quilt started for each person! The quilters gather around tables with rotary cutters, mats, and rulers to cut fabrics into strips. When the bee is over, each person will have enough strips to make a quilt!

Participants bring about 10 to 15 yards of assorted fabrics in an agreed-upon color scheme or theme. Armed with rotary-cutting supplies and a container for holding their fabric strips, the quilters start the day cutting and conversing until everyone has a box that's brimming with fabric strips. A potluck lunch or dinner is an excellent way to take a break in the action or to end the day in celebration of the fruits of your labor.

There are numerous benefits of participating in a Cutting Bee. By sharing fabrics with friends, you don't have to unfold and press dozens of your own fabrics just to cut a few pieces from each. Instead, each friend brings fabric to the bee, cuts the same size strips as

This well-stocked bin contains everything you need for the day: fabric, sewing and cutting supplies, clothespins for sorting cut pieces, and munchies.

the other participants, and then trades strips. Working together to cut the fabrics is quite simply more fun! Swapping with your friends also yields a wider assortment of prints for everyone.

Perhaps one of the biggest benefits of a Cutting Bee is the camaraderie. In today's busy world, how often do you have time to quilt with your friends? A Cutting Bee is a special time planned specifically for that very purpose.

Several quilts in this book are appropriate for a Cutting Bee—The Simple Cross, Jacob's Ladder, Flock of Geese,

and Turnstile. Or you can refer to the other block ideas on page 164 to choose a design that's right for you. Even if you can't get a Cutting Bee together, you can still make these quilts. Just cut the number of strips indicated from your own fabric collection.

We hope you try this fun idea with your friends. It makes a great activity for quilting retreats, too. A Cutting Bee—filled with fabrics, food, fellowship, and fun—is an activity that you and your friends are sure to want to repeat often!

Organizing Your Own Cutting Bee

The idea of a Cutting Bee is to benefit everyone involved by getting a quilt started for each person. Armed with rotary-cutting supplies and fabrics to share, you spend the day cutting and conversing. If you agree that a Cutting Bee sounds like a great idea, here's how to organize your own.

Getting Ready for the Big Day

1. Establish the group. Six to eight participants work well.

2. Set date, time, and place. Make sure you'll have plenty of room for cutting mats and supplies. Consider asking your local library or church if you can use a room.

3. Choose a fabric theme. Agree upon a fabric theme or style so that all fabrics will coordinate. Consider such themes as Americana or Christmas, or go with specific fabrics such as geometrics or floral prints. Several fabrics from a specific line also make good Cutting Bee choices.

4. Decide on an amount for each person to bring. For a bed-size quilt, each person should bring a total of 10 to 12 yards. This should be in half-yard or one-yard pieces.

5. Send out invitations. Give each participant detailed instructions about which fabrics and supplies to bring.

6. Do your homework. Before the event, gather your supplies. You'll need a storage container to hold the strips that you will collect at the Cutting Bee. Clothespins come in handy for holding cut pieces together while in transit.

- Select the agreed-upon amounts from your fabric collection or purchase fabrics in the chosen theme.
- Include light, medium, and dark fabrics.
- Don't get in a stingy, fabric-hoarding mood. Remember, you'll bring home as much as you take. Also, if you contribute nothing but your ugliest fabrics, you may not be asked to participate again!
- Prepare your dish, if your group is having a potluck meal.

Here's How It Works!

First, have each participant cut 2 (4½"-wide) and 3 (2½"-wide) strips from each half-yard piece of fabric. Have everyone place all cut strips on a table.

When everyone is finished cutting, line up and circle around the table, picking up one strip from each pile. Continue circling the table until all the strips are gone.

Next, choose a block design and cut strips into 2½" and 4½" squares and half-square triangles as needed. Participants can trade cut pieces again if more of one color is needed to create a balanced look in the blocks.

After you've cut enough pieces for a few blocks, begin sewing. Have fun talking, laughing, and experimenting with the fabrics. Everyone should be able to make at least one block before the day is over.

Cutting Bee Checklist

Fabric
Large cutting mat
Rotary cutter with new blade
Rulers (6" × 24", 6" × 12", 6" square, Fons & Porter Half & Quarter ruler)
Storage container for cut pieces
Sewing machine
Basic sewing kit
Food

Block Options

These block patterns use units cut from 2½"- and 4½"-wide strips using the Fons & Porter Half & Quarter Ruler as shown on page 165. Large triangles and large squares are cut from 4½"-wide strips. Small triangles and small squares are cut from 2½"-wide strips. The cut size of the rectangles in *Puss in the Corner* is 2½" × 4½". The cut size of the inner rectangles in *The Simple Cross* is 2½" × 4½"; the outer rectangles are cut 2½" × 8½".

8" Blocks

Old Maid's
Puzzle I

Old Maid's
Puzzle II

World's Fair

Flock of Geese

X Quartet

Free Trade

Puss in the
Corner

Lady of the
Lake

Crosses and
Losses I

Crosses and
Losses II

Anvil

12" Blocks

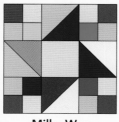
Milky Way

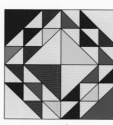
Corn and Beans

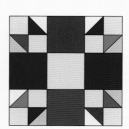
Duck Tracks

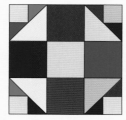
Hens and Chicks

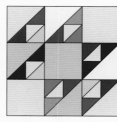
Cat's Cradle

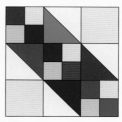
Rocky Road

Cutting Half-Square and Quarter-Square Triangles

Easily cut half-square and quarter-square triangles from strips of the same width with the Fons & Porter Half & Quarter Ruler.

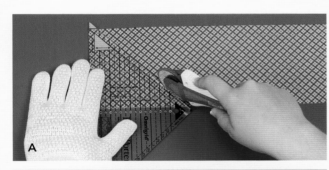

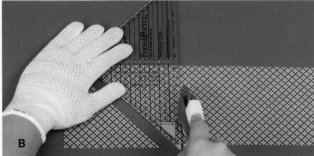

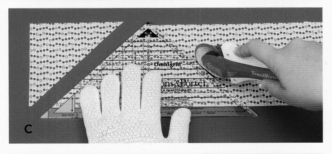

Cutting Half-Square Triangles

1. Straighten the left edge of 4½"-wide fabric strip. Place the 4½" line of the Fons & Porter Half & Quarter Ruler on the bottom edge of strip, aligning left edge of ruler with straightened edge of strip. The yellow tip of ruler will extend beyond top edge of strip.

2. Cut along right edge of ruler to make 1 half-square triangle (*Photo A*).

3. Turn ruler and align 4½" line with top edge of strip. Cut along right edge of ruler (*Photo B*).

4. Repeat to cut required number of half-square triangles.

Cutting Quarter-Square Triangles

1. Place Fons & Porter Half & Quarter Ruler on 4½"-wide fabric strip, with 4½" line along bottom edge. The black tip of ruler will extend beyond top edge. Trim off end of strip along left edge of ruler.

2. Cut along right edge of ruler to make 1 quarter-square triangle (*Photo C*).

3. Turn ruler and align 4½" line along top edge of strip. Cut along right edge of ruler (*Photo D*).

4. Repeat to cut required number of quarter-square triangles.

General Instructions

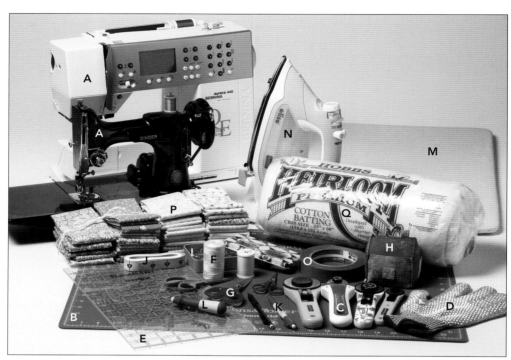

Basic Supplies

You'll need a **sewing machine (A)** in good working order to construct patchwork blocks, join blocks together, add borders, and machine quilt. We encourage you to purchase a machine from a local dealer, who can help you with service in the future, rather than from a discount store. Another option may be to borrow a machine from a friend or family member. If the machine has not been used in a while, have it serviced by a local dealer to make sure it is in good working order. If you need an extension cord, one with a surge protector is a good idea.

A **rotary cutting mat (B)** is essential for accurate and safe rotary cutting. Purchase one that is no smaller than 18" × 24". Rotary cutting mats are made of "self-healing" material that can be used over and over.

A **rotary cutter (C)** is a cutting tool that looks like a pizza cutter, and has a very sharp blade. We recommend starting with a standard size 45mm rotary cutter. Always lock or close your cutter when it is not in use, and keep it out of the reach of children.

A **safety glove** (also known as a *Klutz Glove)* **(D)** is also recommended. Wear your safety glove on the hand that is holding the ruler in place. Because it is made of cut-resistant material, the safety glove protects your non-cutting hand from accidents that can occur if your cutting hand slips while cutting.

An acrylic **ruler (E)** is used in combination with your cutting mat and rotary cutter. We recommend the Fons & Porter 8" × 14" ruler, but a 6" × 12" ruler is another good option. You'll need a ruler with inch, quarter-inch, and eighth-inch markings that show clearly for ease of measuring. Choose a ruler with a 45-degree and 60-degree angle lines marked on it as well.

Since you will be using 100% cotton fabric for your quilts, use **cotton or cotton-covered polyester thread (F)** for piecing and quilting. Avoid 100% polyester thread, as it tends to snarl.

Keep a pair of small **scissors (G)** near your sewing machine for cutting threads.

Thin, good quality **straight pins (H)** are preferred by quilters. The pins included with pin cushions are normally too thick to

¼ yard versus Fat Quarter

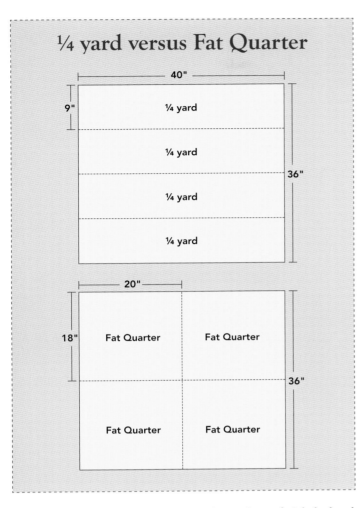

The most exciting item that you will need for quilting is **fabric (P)**. Quilters generally prefer 100% cotton fabrics for their quilts. This fabric is woven from cotton threads, and has a lengthwise and a crosswise grain. The term "bias" is used to describe the diagonal grain of the fabric. If you make a 45-degree angle cut through a square of cotton fabric, the cut edges will be bias edges, which are quite stretchy. As you learn more quiltmaking techniques, you'll learn how bias can work to your advantage or disadvantage.

Fabric is sold by the yard at quilt shops and fabric stores. Quilting fabric is generally about 40"–44" wide, so a yard is about 40" wide by 36" long. As you collect fabrics to build your own personal stash, you will buy yards, half yards (about 40" × 18"), quarter yards (about 40" × 9"), as well as other lengths.

Many quilt shops sell "fat quarters," a special cut favored by quilters. A fat quarter is created by cutting a half yard down the fold line into two 20" × 18" pieces (fat quarters) that are sold separately. Quilters like the nearly square shape of the fat quarter because it is more useful than the narrow regular quarter-yard cut.

Batting (Q) is the filler between quilt top and backing that makes your quilt a quilt. It can be cotton, polyester, cotton-polyester blend, wool, silk, or other natural materials, such as bamboo or corn. Make sure the batting you buy is at least six inches wider and six inches longer than your quilt top.

use for piecing, so discard them. Purchase a box of nickel-plated brass **safety pins** size #1 **(I)** to use for pin-basting the layers of your quilt together for machine quilting.

Invest in a 120"-long dressmaker's **measuring tape (J)**. This will come in handy when making borders for your quilt.

A 0.7–0.9mm mechanical **pencil (K)** works well for marking on your fabric.

Invest in a quality sharp **seam ripper (L)**. Every quilter gets well-acquainted with her seam ripper!

Set up an **ironing board (M)** and **iron (N)** in your sewing area. Pressing yardage before cutting, and pressing patchwork seams as you go are both essential for quality quiltmaking. Select an iron that has steam capability.

Masking **tape (O)** or painter's tape works well to mark your sewing machine so you can sew an accurate ¼" seam. You will also use tape to hold your backing fabric taut as you prepare your quilt sandwich for machine quilting.

Accurate Cutting

Measuring and cutting accuracy are important for successful quilting. Measure at least twice, and cut once!

Cutting for patchwork usually begins with cutting strips, which are then cut into smaller pieces. First, cut straight strips from a fat quarter:

1. Fold fat quarter in half with selvage edge at the top (*Photo A*).

2. Straighten edge of fabric by placing ruler atop fabric, aligning one of the lines on ruler with selvage edge of fabric (*Photo B*). Cut along right edge of ruler.

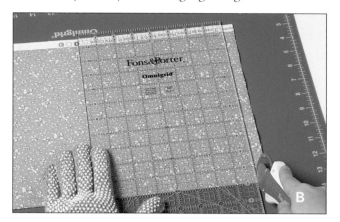

3. Rotate fabric, and use ruler to measure from cut edge to desired strip width (*Photo C*). Measurements in instructions include ¼" seam allowances.

Setting up Your Sewing Machine

Sew Accurate ¼" Seams

Standard seam width for patchwork and quiltmaking is ¼". Some machines come with a patchwork presser foot, also known as a quarter-inch foot. If your machine doesn't have a quarter-inch foot, you may be able to purchase one from a dealer. Or, you can create a quarter-inch seam guide on your machine using masking tape or painter's tape.

Place an acrylic ruler on your sewing machine bed under the presser foot. Slowly turn handwheel until the tip of the needle barely rests atop the ruler's quarter-inch mark (*Photo A*). Make sure the lines on the ruler are parallel to the lines on the machine throat plate. Place tape on the machine bed along edge of ruler (*Photo B*).

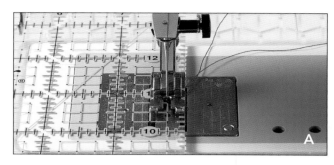

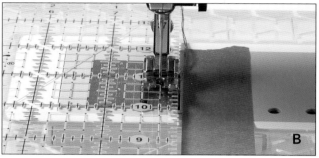

Take a Simple Seam Test

Seam accuracy is critical to machine piecing, so take this simple test once you have your quarter-inch presser foot on your machine or have created a tape guide.

Place 2 (2½") squares right sides together, and sew with a scant ¼" seam. Open squares and finger press seam. To finger press, with right sides facing you, press the seam to one side with your fingernail. Measure across pieces, raw edge to raw edge (*Photo C*). If they measure 4½", you have passed the test! Repeat the test as needed to make sure you can confidently sew a perfect ¼" seam.

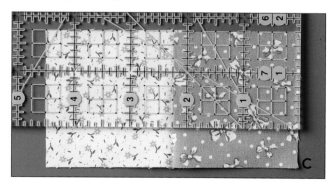

Sewing Comfortably

Other elements that promote pleasant sewing are good lighting, a comfortable chair, background music—and chocolate! Good lighting promotes accurate sewing. The better you can see what you are working on, the better your results. A comfortable chair enables you to sew for longer periods of time. An office chair with a good back rest and adjustable height works well. Music helps keep you relaxed. Chocolate is, for many quilters, simply a necessity.

Tips for Patchwork and Pressing

As you sew more patchwork, you'll develop your own shortcuts and favorite methods. Here are a few favored by many quilters:

● As you join patchwork units to form rows, and join rows to form blocks, press seams in opposite directions from row to row whenever possible (*Photo A*). By pressing seams one direction in the first row and the opposite direction in the next row, you will often create seam allowances that abut when rows are joined (*Photo B*). Abutting or nesting seams are ideal for forming perfectly matched corners on the right side of your quilt blocks and quilt top. Such pressing is not always possible, so don't worry if you end up with seam allowances facing the same direction as you join units.

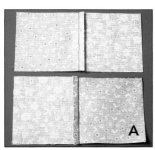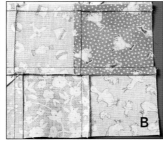

● Sew on and off a small, folded fabric square to prevent bobbin thread from bunching at throat plate (*Photo C*). You'll also save thread, which means fewer stops to wind bobbins, and fewer hanging threads to be snipped. Repeated use of the small piece of fabric gives it lots of thread "legs," so some quilters call it a spider.

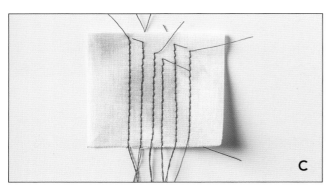

● Chain piece patchwork to reduce the amount of thread you use, and minimize the number and length of threads you need to trim from patchwork. Without cutting threads at the end of a seam, take 3–4 stitches without any fabric under the needle, creating a short thread chain approximately ⅛" long (*Photo D*). Repeat until you have a long line of pieces. Remove chain from machine, clip threads between units, and press seams.

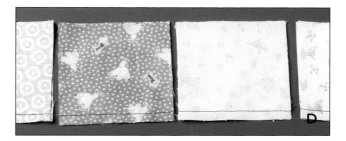

● Trim off tiny triangle tips (sometimes called dog ears) created when making triangle-square units (*Photo E*). Trimming triangles reduces bulk and makes patchwork units and blocks lie flatter. Though no one will see the back of your quilt top once it's quilted, a neat back free of dangling threads and patchwork points is the mark of a good quilter. Also, a smooth, flat quilt top is easier to quilt, whether by hand or machine.

● Careful pressing will make your patchwork neat and crisp, and will help make your finished quilt top lie flat. Ironing and pressing are two different skills. Iron fabric to remove wrinkles using a back and forth, smoothing motion. Press patchwork and quilt blocks by raising and gently lowering the iron atop your work. After sewing a patchwork unit, first press the seam with the unit closed, pressing to set, or embed, the stitching. Setting the seam this way will help produce straight, crisp seams. Open the unit and press on the right side with the seam toward the darkest fabric, being careful to not form a pleat in your seam, and carefully pressing the patchwork flat.

- Many quilters use finger pressing to open and flatten seams of small units before pressing with an iron. To finger press, open patchwork unit with right side of fabric facing you. Run your fingernail firmly along seam, making sure unit is fully open with no pleat.

- Careful use of steam in your iron will make seams and blocks crisp and flat (*Photo F*). Aggressive ironing can stretch blocks out of shape, and is a common pitfall for new quilters.

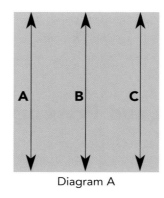

Diagram A

A _____
B _____
C _____

TOTAL _____

_____ ÷3

AVERAGE LENGTH _____

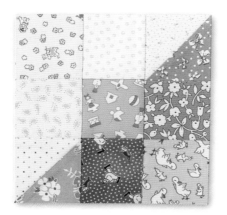

F

Adding Borders

Follow these simple instructions to make borders that fit perfectly on your quilt.

1. Find the length of your quilt by measuring through the quilt center, not along the edges, since the edges may have stretched. Take 3 measurements and average them to determine the length to cut your side borders (*Diagram A*). Cut 2 side borders this length.

2. Fold border strips in half to find center. Pinch to create crease mark or place a pin at center. Fold quilt top in half crosswise to find center of side. Attach side borders to quilt center by pinning them at the ends and the center, and easing in any fullness. If quilt edge is a bit longer than border, pin and sew with border on top; if border is slightly longer than quilt top, pin and sew with border on the bottom. Machine feed dogs will ease in the fullness of the longer piece. Press seams toward borders.

HELPFUL TIP

Use the following decimal conversions to calculate your quilt's measurements:

$\frac{1}{8}$" = .125	$\frac{5}{8}$" = .625
$\frac{1}{4}$" = .25	$\frac{3}{4}$" = .75
$\frac{3}{8}$" = .375	$\frac{7}{8}$" = .875
$\frac{1}{2}$" = .5	

3. Find the width of your quilt by measuring across the quilt and side borders (*Diagram B*). Take 3 measurements and average them to determine the length to cut your top and bottom borders. Cut 2 borders this length.

4. Mark centers of borders and top and bottom edges of quilt top. Attach top and bottom borders to quilt, pinning at ends and center, and easing in any fullness (*Diagram C*). Press seams toward borders.

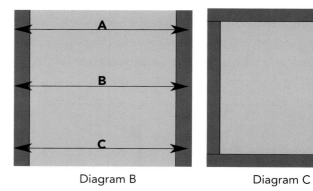

Diagram B   Diagram C

5. Gently steam press entire quilt top on one side and then the other. When pressing on wrong side, trim off any loose threads.

Joining Border Strips

Not all quilts have borders, but they are a nice complement to a quilt top. If your border is longer than 40", you will need to join 2 or more strips to make a border the required length. You can join border strips with either a straight seam parallel to the ends of the strips (*Photo A*), or with a diagonal seam (*Photo B*). For the diagonal seam method, place one border strip perpendicular to another strip, rights sides facing. Stitch diagonally across strips as shown. Trim seam allowance to ¼". Press seam open (*Photo C*).

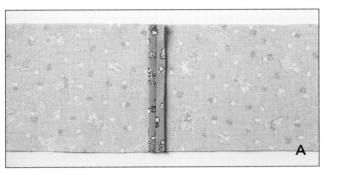

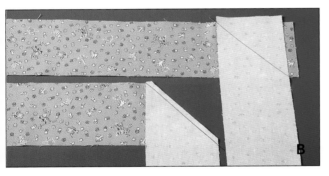

Quilting Your Quilt

Quilters today joke that there are three ways to quilt a quilt— by hand, by machine, or by check. Some enjoy making quilt tops so much, they prefer to hire a professional machine quilter to finish their work.

Decide what color thread will look best on your quilt top before choosing your backing fabric. A thread color that will blend in with the quilt top is a good choice for beginners. Choose backing fabric that will blend with your thread as well. A print fabric is a good choice for hiding less-than-perfect machine quilting. The backing fabric must be at least 3"–4" larger than your quilt top on all 4 sides. For example: if your quilt top measures 44" × 44", your backing needs to be at least 50" × 50". If your quilt top is 80" × 96", then your backing fabric needs to be at least 86" × 102".

For quilt tops 36" wide or less, use a single width of fabric for the backing. Buy enough length to allow adequate margin at quilt edges, as noted above. When your quilt is wider than 36", one option is to use 60"-, 90"-, or 108"-wide fabric for the quilt backing. Because fabric selection is limited for wide fabrics, quilters generally piece the quilt backing from 44/45"-wide fabric. Plan on 40"–42" of usable fabric width when estimating how much fabric to purchase. Plan your piecing strategy to avoid having a seam along the veritcal or horizontal center of the quilt.

For a quilt 37"–60" wide, a backing with horizontal seams is usually the most economical use of fabric. For example, for a quilt 50" × 70", vertical seams would require 152", or 4¼ yards, of 44/45"-wide fabric (76" + 76" = 152"). Horizontal seams would require 112", or 3¼ yards (56" + 56" = 112").

For a quilt 61"–80" wide, most quilters piece a three-panel backing, with vertical seams, from two lengths of fabric. Cut one of the pieces in half lengthwise, and sew the halves to opposite sides of the wider panel. Press the seams away from the center panel.

| Horizontal Seam Back | Three Panel Backing | Offset Seam |

For a quilt 81"–120" wide, you will need three lengths of fabric, plus extra margin. For example, for a quilt 108" × 108", purchase at least 342", or 9½ yards, of 44/45"-wide fabric (114" + 114" + 114" = 342").

For a three-panel backing, pin the selvage edge of the enter panel to the selvage edge of the side panel, with edges aligned and right sides facing. Machine stitch with a ½" seam. Trim seam allowances to ¼", trimming off the selvages from both panels at once. Press the seam away from the center of the quilt. Repeat on other side of center panel.

For a two-panel backing, join panels in the same manner as above, and press the seam to one side.

Create a "quilt sandwich" by layering your backing, batting, and quilt top. Find the cross-wise center of the backing fabric by folding it in half. Mark with a pin on each side. Lay backing down on a table or floor, wrong side up. Tape corners and edges of backing to the surface with masking or painter's tape so that backing is taut (*Photo A*).

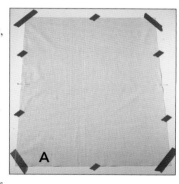

Fold batting in half crosswise and position it atop backing fabric, centering folded edge at center of backing (*Photo B*). Unfold batting and smooth it out atop backing (*Photo C*).

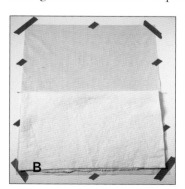

In the same manner, fold the quilt top in half crosswise and center it atop backing and batting (*Photo D*). Unfold top and smooth it out atop batting (*Photo E*).

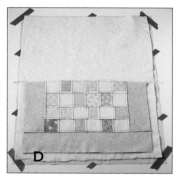

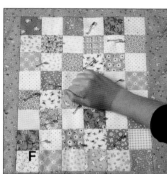

Use safety pins to pin baste the layers (*Photo F*). Pins should be about a fist width apart. A special tool, called a Kwik Klip, or a grapefruit spoon makes closing the pins easier. As you slide a pin through all three layers, slide the point of the pin into one of the tool's grooves. Push on the tool to help close the pin.

For straight line quilting, install an even feed or walking foot on your machine. This presser foot helps all three layers of your quilt move through the machine evenly without bunching.

| Walking Foot | Stitching "in the ditch" |

An easy way to quilt your first quilt is to stitch "in the ditch" along seam lines. No marking is needed for this type of quilting.

Binding Your Quilt

Preparing Binding

Strips for quilt binding may be cut either on the straight of grain or on the bias. For the quilts in this book, cut strips on the straight of grain unless otherwise noted.

1. Measure the perimeter of your quilt and add approximately 24" to allow for mitered corners and finished ends.

2. Cut the number of strips necessary to achieve desired length. We like to cut binding strips 2¼" wide.

3. Join your strips with diagonal seams into 1 continuous piece (*Photo A*). Press the seams open. (See page 171 for instructions for the diagonal seams method of joining strips.)

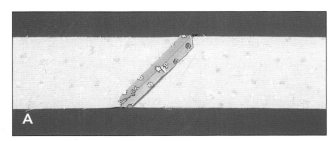

4. Press your binding in half lengthwise, with wrong sides facing, to make French-fold binding (*Photo B*).

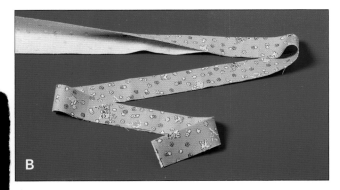

Attaching Binding

Attach the binding to your quilt using an even-feed or walking foot. This prevents puckering when sewing through the three layers.

1. Choose beginning point along one side of quilt. Do not start at a corner. Match the two raw edges of the binding strip to the raw edge of the quilt top. The folded edge will be free and to left of seam line (*Photo C*). Leave 12" or longer tail of binding strip dangling free from beginning point. Stitch, using ¼" seam, through all layers.

2. For mitered corners, stop stitching ¼" from corner; backstitch, and remove quilt from sewing machine (*Photo D*). Place a pin ¼" from corner to mark where you will stop stitching.

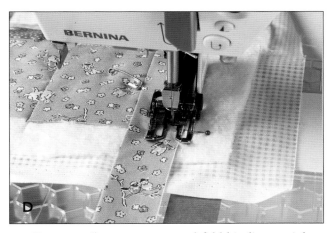

Rotate quilt quarter turn and fold binding straight up, away from corner, forming 45-degree-angle fold (*Photo E*).

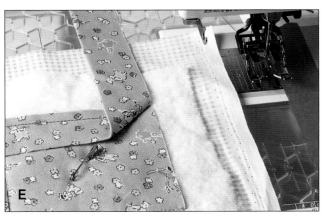

Bring binding straight down in line with next edge to be sewn, leaving top fold even with raw edge of previously sewn side (*Photo F*). Begin stitching at top edge, sewing through all layers (*Photo G*).

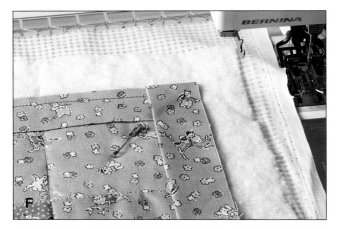

3. To finish binding, stop stitching about 8" away from starting point, leaving about a 12" tail at end (*Photo H*). Bring beginning and end of binding to center of 8" opening and fold each back, leaving about ¼" space

between the two folds of binding (*Photo I*). (Allowing this ¼" extra space is critical, as binding tends to stretch when it is stitched to the quilt. If the folded ends meet at this point, your binding will be too long for the space after the ends are joined.) Crease folds of binding with your fingernail.

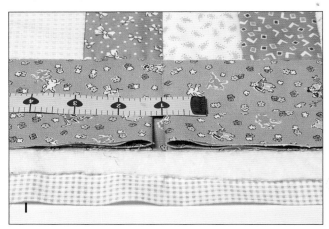

4. Open out each edge of binding and draw line across wrong side of binding on creased fold line, as shown in *Photo J*. Draw line along lengthwise fold of binding at same spot to create an X (*Photo K*).

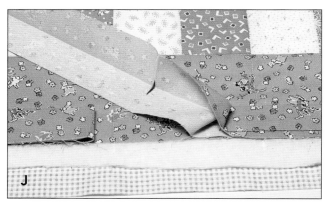

5. With edge of ruler at marked X, line up 45-degree-angle marking on ruler with one long side of binding (*Photo L*). Draw diagonal line across binding as shown in *Photo M*.

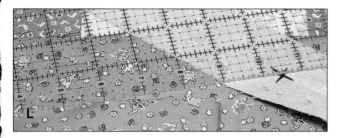

Repeat for other end of binding. Lines must angle in same direction (*Photo N*).

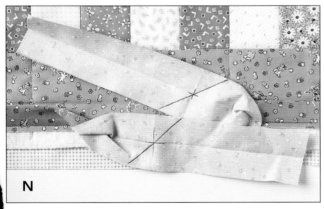

6. Pin binding ends together with right sides facing, pin-matching diagonal lines as shown in *Photo O*. Binding ends will be at right angles to each other. Machine-stitch along diagonal line, removing pins as you stitch (*Photo P*).

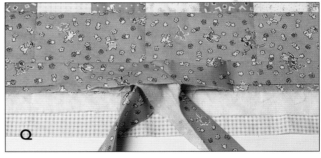

7. Lay binding against quilt to double-check that it is correct length (*Photo Q*). Trim ends of binding ¼" from diagonal seam (*Photo R*).

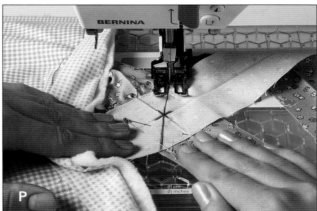

8. Finger press diagonal seam open (*Photo S*). Fold binding in half and finish stitching binding to quilt (*Photo T*).

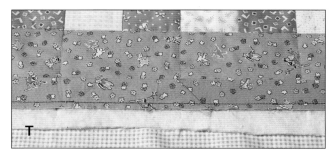

Hand Stitching Binding to Quilt Back

1. Trim any excess batting and quilt back with scissors or a rotary cutter (*Photo A*). Leave enough batting (about ⅛" beyond quilt top) to fill binding uniformly when it is turned to quilt back.

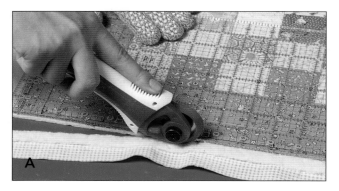

2. Bring folded edge of binding to quilt back so that it covers machine stitching. Blindstitch folded edge to quilt backing, using a few pins just ahead of stitching to hold binding in place (*Photo B*).

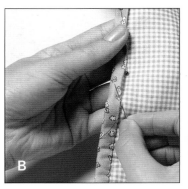

3. Continue stitching to corner. Fold unstitched binding from next side under, forming a 45-degree angle and a mitered corner. Stitch mitered folds on both front and back (*Photo C*).

Finishing Touches

- **Label your quilt so the recipient and future generations know who made it.** To make a label, use a fabric marking pen to write the details on a small piece of solid color fabric (*Photo A*). To make writing easier, put pieces of masking tape on the wrong side. Remove tape after writing. Use your iron to turn under ¼" on each edge, then stitch the label to the back of your quilt using a blindstitch, taking care not to sew through to quilt top.

- **Take a photo of your quilt.** Keep your photos in an album or journal along with notes, fabric swatches, and other information about the quilts.

- **If your quilt is a gift, include care instructions.** Some quilt shops carry pre-printed care labels you can sew onto the quilt (*Photo B*). Or, make a care label using the method described above.